Elizabeth Edson Evans

The Abuse of Maternity

Elizabeth Edson Evans

The Abuse of Maternity

ISBN/EAN: 9783742816719

Manufactured in Europe, USA, Canada, Australia, Japa

Cover: Foto ©Thomas Meinert / pixelio.de

Manufactured and distributed by brebook publishing software
(www.brebook.com)

Elizabeth Edson Evans

The Abuse of Maternity

THE

ABUSE OF MATERNITY.

BY

ELIZABETH EDSON EVANS.

PHILADELPHIA:

J. B. LIPPINCOTT & CO.

1875.

CONTENTS.

PART I.

PART II.

THE ABUSE OF MATERNITY.

PART I.

THROUGH ITS REJECTION.

" How few people, if they had sufficient acquaintance with the nature of the human mind to calculate the sufferings consequent on crime, would ever commit it! And how necessary it must be to educate them into this acquaintance, and to dissipate the ignorance that veils the future from their view."

MRS. CROWE.

THE ABUSE OF MATERNITY.

THE strongest human tie is, undoubtedly, that which binds a mother to her child. In asserting this principle, the writer would not undervalue that wonderful sentiment which makes the lover, although a comparative stranger, all in all to the maiden's heart; nor lose sight of those instances where conjugal sympathy is so absorbing and complete that children are not longed for, and, if they come, are secondary objects of interest to the wife as well as to the husband.

In the first case, the passion, in its height, is temporary, depending for its continuance in a calmer form upon the worth of its object; cases of the second kind are exceptional, presupposing an elevation of intellect and a harmony of sentiment extremely rare. Maternal devotion, on the other hand, is a universal instinct, independent alike of the cultivation of the affections and of the development of the intellectual powers, as well as undismayed by any degree of ingratitude and depravity in its recipient.

7

No woman can be considered as having com-
pleted her destiny until she has borne a child.
She may live honored and beloved as a perpetual
daughter in her father's house; as a childless wife,
she may be better to her husband than ten sons;
her published words may exert a world-wide influence for good, and her personal presence may have
power as an angel of healing in hospital and camp;
she may feel and acknowledge that it is better for
her fellows that she has been left free to work in
an extended sphere; and yet—and yet—however
highly she may be prized in private or in public
life, she is pitied as one who has either missed,
or voluntarily resigned, the dearest privilege of her
sex; and, in her secret heart, although she may
be resigned, and even content, she can never be
satisfied.

All this being true, it seems at first sight unac-
countably strange that there should exist, nay, that
there should always have existed, in all countries
and under all degrees of civilization, a disposition
on the part of women to evade the task of maternity, and that this disposition should have resulted
in the prevalence of *fœticide*,—a practice so unnatural, so cowardly, so cruel and unjust, that it
has well been denominated "the nameless crime."

In the occasional protests against this sin which
appear in our public journals of the present day,
it is generally alluded to as a modern vice, an
outgrowth of French civilization, transplanted to

America to minister to the growing passion for the luxurious ease and refined sensuality which characterize fashionable society in Paris. But the temptation is probably as old as the race, and it is doubtful whether there were ever a people among whom the deed was utterly unknown, or a period wherein it was not performed.

There can be no effect without an adequate cause; therefore there must be sufficient reasons for the long-continued existence of a practice which does not claim any higher motive than expediency, and which the most enlightened minds in every age have deplored and condemned.

The principal reason, no doubt, has always been an excess of population. The misery experienced by the poorer classes, whenever the demand for the necessaries of life exceeds the supply, invariably tends not only to tempt the sufferers to lighten their burden in this summary manner, but to hinder the action of legislation, and induce philanthropists and political economists to look upon the crime as a necessary evil, if not a doubtful good. It is the pressure of poverty, and not the absence of the maternal instinct, that leads the mothers of China, India, and Japan to expose and slay the majority of their offspring. The fallacy of the proverb that "God never sends a mouth without food to put into it," is amply proved among the teeming millions of those fruitful lands; and until the only natural and innocent check to our over-population be adopted, the unnatural and criminal check will be resorted to, with more or less of the conviction that the end sanctifies the means.

Indeed, there has always existed in many minds an honest doubt whether, under certain circumstances, the deed be really criminal. Thus, Ovid, Juvenal, and Seneca, writing as poets and moralists, condemn it as a sin and a disgrace; but Plato and Aristotle, as philosophers and political economists, advise it as a means not only of keeping down population, but of improving the race by including among the destroyed all maimed and deformed infants, and suffering no child to be born alive after the mother is over forty, or the father over fifty-five, years of age. Doubtless these wise men would have preferred that propagation should be self-restrained within proper limits and favorable conditions; but they knew that the citizens of their ideal states must be taken from the world as it is, and so they shaped their laws accordingly.

The same recognition of facts as triumphant over theories is displayed in the economical regulations of the Germans of Scandinavia and Iceland in ancient times. In Iceland, when the annual yield of provisions could be closely calculated, the population was nicely adjusted to the quantity of food; and not only were infants exposed without hesitation, but old people, and other persons who, from any cause, were incapable of earning a livelihood, were killed to make room for the young

and the active. Marriage was forbidden, unless
the contracting parties were possessed of sufficient
property to support a family; and those who ventured to evade this law were banished at once
from the country, together with all persons who
had abetted the union or taken part in the cere-
mony, unless these last agreed to take upon themselves the nourishment of any children that might
be born to the improvident pair. When the inhabitants decided to accept Christianity as the
national religion, it was done with two provisions,
namely, that the people should continue to be
allowed to eat horse-flesh, and to expose their
children. In the other Scandinavian countries,
where the supply of food was not so limited,
child-murder was forbidden from the very introduction of Christianity; and it is but just to say
that even in Iceland, and before the overthrow of
Paganism, the progress of civilization had wrought
upon the better instincts of the people to such a
degree that the exposure of infants was practiced
with constantly-increasing reluctance, so that the
proviso above mentioned would seem to have been
instituted rather to prevent punishment in cases of
extreme necessity, than to give free course to the
cruel impulses of a barbarous people.

But various other causes, besides the pressure of
poverty, have been able to pervert the human
conscience with reference to the rights of unborn
and new-born children.

Until within a comparatively recent period, there existed in Otaheite and the neighboring islands a society, the chief object of which was the destruction at birth of all the children of members. The constitution of this society has never been 'discovered, but the practice is supposed to have originated in some religious principle. The members were persons distinguished by valor and merit, each family of the chiefs being represented by one or more of their best men, while only women of the higher ranks were allowed to join. The society wielded great influence in the community, and the individuals composing it were regarded with the utmost trust and reverence by all classes of the people. In this case, it is supposed that the infants were strangled at birth, and the deed was performed by the members themselves, no attendants being allowed to be present, since this would thereby render themselves liable to be put to death as accessories to murder. Occasionally a mother would relent and wish to spare her child, but in general the women agreed with the men as to the propriety of the sacrifice. One example is related of a chief who had married a sister of the king of Otaheite, and who, after having destroyed eight children born to him, finally adopted a nephew as his heir.

In Turkey, abortion has for ages been practiced with impunity, and to such an extent that the population has been sensibly affected thereby;

and in all Mohammedan communities it is not considered criminal to destroy the fœtus, provided the master of the household has given his consent to the deed. The great number of children that usually pertain to polygamous families, and the lack of an exclusive bond of interest between the parents, no doubt contributed to make both men and women careless of the type.

But in all ages, and among all races and classes, it is probable that the cases wherein the least hesitation at committing this crime would be felt, are those where an illegitimate birth is in question. All people, everywhere, agree in the desirableness of unsullied virginity in the female before marriage; and, where there has been a failure in this particular, it is for the interest of many besides the culprit that all tokens of the fault be secretly done away with. In the days when the exposure of new-born infants was a matter of frequent occurrence, neither protested against by conscience nor forbidden by law, there was less temptation to the practice of fœticide, which was seldom resorted to excepting in the case of pregnancy before marriage. But with the gradual enlightenment of public opinion arose the necessity of greater privacy in the management of these deeds of darkness, and there followed, consequently, an increase in the number of pre-natal victims.

There is no doubt that the crime of fœticide

has been committed by thousands of persons who would have shrunk with horror from laying violent hands upon a breathing child. And this distinction has been made, not alone because, in the one case, the absence of a visible object prevented a full realization of the nature of the wrong, but because of the existence of an honest belief that, prior to the period of "quickening," the child in the womb has no "life," and may be separated from the parent-body like any inconvenient or hurtful excrescence. The natural sensations of prospective mothers have fostered this erroneous judgment, since only those who have ardently desired offspring can say with truth that, from the moment they were conscious of being pregnant, the embryo was to them as important and as dear as during those later months when its motions had become a constant reminder of its speedy appearance as an independent being. The disagreeable, and often painful, disturbance of physical health, together with the unusual excitement of mind consequent upon so great a revolution in the system, generally make of the first months of pregnancy a period of alarm and unrest, offering few or no suggestions of the bliss to follow, and the patient's instinctive impulse is to free herself from the thraldom of the new and undefined power which has taken such firm hold of the very sources of her being. The sense of responsibility is not yet awakened, and the sacredness of indi-

viduality is seriously intruded upon by the consciousness of a second existence running parallel
with her own.

Legislation, too, has, until recently, given some
countenance to the crime, by the nice distinctions
made in the offense according to the period of its
committal. Thus, in the former penal code of
Great Britain, while the enactments against infanticide were extremely severe, and often unjust
in their working (a state of things of which Sir
Walter Scott has made a fine use in his trial of
Effie Deans), abortion was considered murder only
when it was induced after the quickening of the
fœtus, and in Scotland it was punished as homicide
only in case of the death of the mother. But, in
the latter part of the reign of William the Fourth
and the first of the reign of Victoria, the laws were
modified; evidence was appointed to be taken in
cases of suspected infanticide, as in other instances
of murder, and all who should be concerned in
procuring abortion at any stage of pregnancy, or
by any means, were adjudged guilty of felony, to
be punished by death or transportation, according
to the circumstances of the case.

In this matter, as in many others, the ancient
code of the Parsis sets a good example to modern
legislation. The "Vendidad" contains the following
statute: "The maiden, whether betrothed or un-
betrothed, who becomes pregnant, is forbidden to
injure the fruit of her body, on account of a feeling

of shame before men. She who thus injures the
fruit of her body, commits a sin against her parents,
and shall atone for it by death. If the man say to
her, 'Make friends with an old woman and ask her
to help you,' and if the old woman bring any destructive plant, saying, 'Take this to kill the child,'
and if the maiden take the medicine for this purpose, then the man, the maiden, and the old woman
(the abortionist) are equally culpable." A misun-
derstanding of this passage led the missionary, J.
Wilson, in his book, "The Parsi Religion Un-
folded," p. 80, to charge the Zarathustra with
inculcating and commanding the practice of fœticide. The charge is wholly groundless, as is
clearly evident from the context.

Among the Scandinavians in ancient times,
although new-born children were exposed with
impunity, yet if water were once poured upon an
infant, or a drop of nourishment had touched its
lips, its life was considerd sacred, and violence,
though committed the moment after, became
murder.

And now, medical authorities everywhere recognize the fact that life begins to each human germ
with the instant of conception, and law everywhere
professes to consider abortion as murder; although
the general public is still misled, through the pro-
mulgation by unprincipled charlatans of false and
obsolete theories, and justice is comparatively in-
operative against a practice which, being always

conducted with the greatest possible secrecy, is, in most cases, exceedingly difficult of detection.

If there be a people who are, and always have been, exempt from blood-guiltiness with respect to fœtal life, it is the Jews. Indeed, the crime of murder in any shape is of singularly rare occurrence among them, as may easily be seen by reference to statistics in every part of the world where they have found a home. A horror of shedding blood has been instilled into the whole race from the time of Moses, the spirit of whose code, so far as domestic morality is concerned, still governs the people which claims him as its leader and law-giver. The solemn ceremonies accompanying circumcision; the declaration that all that openeth the womb, the first-born óf man and beast, is holy unto the Lord; the minute regulations concerning the purification of women after menstruation and child-birth, and of both sexes after the performance of the act of copulation,—all tended to make the Hebrews appreciative of the sacredness of sexual union, and of the responsibility incurred through the invoking of a new life. No circumstance seems to have been overlooked which could suggest to this newly-emancipated people the tenderness of the parental tie. Even a kid must not be seethed in its mother's milk. The best incitement to obedience and general good conduct on the part of the tribes was the promise that nothing should cast its young nor be barren in their land; and the

3

heaviest of curses upon the impious and unruly was, "They shall be childless : they shall die childless." This endeavor to preserve and strengthen a feeble power through a rapid growth of population was natural at a time when physical force was the chief means for the establishment of a nation ; but the just and merciful ideas thus inculcated in the Hebrew race have survived their loss of nationality and all the vicissitudes which might be supposed to mitigate against a desire of increase in a homeless and persecuted people. To this day, each Jewish family is governed, in its most intimate relations, by a code of minute regulations which are a digest and necessary modification of the laws of Moses and of later accepted teachers. These rules are calculated for the preservation alike of physical health and of moral purity; and some idea of their conscientious strictness may be obtained from the fact that one clause forbids any woman, after having taken part in the procreative act, to bathe herself, so long as any possibility remains that, by so doing, she may destroy what might otherwise result in conception.

It is curious to see how, in the history of every people, this peculiar form of wickedness has resulted from similar causes at corresponding conditions of external circumstances and in the same order of procedure. First, there is the natural cruelty of barbarous and undeveloped human beings against the weak and helpless of their kind, extending even to the fruit of their own bodies, as shown in the custom obtaining among certain savage tribes of burying the living infant with its dead mother, in case of the latter dying in childbirth or during the period of suckling; as, also, in the atrocities committed upon infants and women with child during the wars of ancient times, and in the sacrifice of infants in the ceremonies of religious superstition.

Next comes the making away of the fruit of the womb, in order to avoid the disgrace of violated virginity; a crime which appears with the first organization of civilized society, and accompanies it throughout all its developments and refinements; then follows the general and scarcely-concealed attempt to restrain population within necessary limits through the practice of infanticide and abortion; and, finally, the reckless waste of embryonic and fœtal life at the dictates of fashion and luxurious enervation.

This last form of temptation is the one from which society at the present time has the most to fear. The opening of the whole world to the interchange of commercial advantages, while it tends to the equalization of population, the elimination of barbarous practices in remote nations, and the dissemination of advanced ideas among isolated and ignorant communities, tends also to the promotion of wealth, and the prevalence of luxury with all its attendant vices,—the latest and most

abundant crop of evils which knowledge has to
destroy.

France, which boasts continually of being at
the head and front of civilization, has certainly
distinguished herself as the chief assassin of inno-
cents, born and unborn,—as the most successful
dispenser of means for both the prevention and
the cure of the (so-considered) plague of natural
increase. With a population already deprived of
one whole generation, through the effects of the
later conscriptions of the first Napoleon, her citizens still continue to limit the number of their
offspring according to individual convenience or
caprice; so that while the population of other
civilized nations is steadily increasing, that of
France remains stationary, and in some districts
even shows a tendency to decline. It is impossible
to calculate the evil influences of this example
upon the rest of the world, especially as it is well
known that the smallness of French families is
not due to abstemiousness as regards sexual indulgence; since there is no other country where
lasciviousness is so exalted into an art, and where
invention is so exhausted in order to stimulate the
wearied passions of professed pleasure-seekers.

In Italy, where there is great corruption of
morals, with less of shrewd calculation than belongs to the French character, the women, especially those of the upper and middle classes, have
a very low appreciation of the duties of maternity,

evading, as much as possible, the natural results both of gallantry and of marital intercourse, and, in many cases, not hesitating to employ more active measures where precaution has failed to prove a sufficient safeguard.

Switzerland, which one would like to think of as the home of all just sentiments and hardy virtues, is not entirely exempt from this form of iniquity; and England, where domestic tenderness has crystallized from the language two of the loveliest gems of human speech,—*Mother* and *Home*, —even England is tolerating, with increasing indifference (as appears from the occasional complaints of alarmed and horrified physicians), the secret ravages of the "nameless crime" among the better classes; while with regard to infanticide among the common people, a recent medical authority declares that "the police think no more of finding the dead body of a child in the streets than of picking up a dead cat or dog."

In Germany (as in most countries where it is desirable to keep up the population to the maximum, in order that the "fruit of love" may furnish "food for cannon"), the laws against infanticide and fœticide are very severe, and yet both crimes occur with considerable frequency among the common people of the large cities. There are many private institutions where women of the upper and middle classes may find a temporary retreat and proper care, in the event of their becoming preg-

nant under embarrassing or criminal circumstances,
and notices to this effect are frequently published
in the newspapers ; but there are no advertisements
of abortionists, or of means of abortion ; nor would
it be easy to find a physician willing to risk incur-
ring the penalties of such a deed, however great
might be the temptation or the bribe. It is said,
however, that the midwives who attend upon the
women of the lower orders are less scrupulous,
often inducing parturition at the seventh month,
in which case the child is pretty sure to die ; and,
even where no foul play is practiced, the custom
of sending illegitimate children, a few days after
birth, to the country to be reared by peasants, is
productive of great mortality, these nurses being
so notoriously careless and unsuccessful with their
charges that they are called in derision "angel-
makers."

From this hasty survey of the countries of the
Old World most open to the observation of travel-
ers, let us turn to contemplate the condition of a
nation which stands without precedent, as regards
rapidity of growth in material and intellectual
prosperity and enviable freedom from inherited
hindrances to improvement.

The United States of America,—the Great Republic,—where millions of fertile acres are waiting
for inhabitants, and no relics of past ignorance or
despotism stand as stumbling-blocks in the way of
sons and daughters born to any citizen of "the land

of the free,"—surely here, of all places in the world, children should be welcomed in city and hamlet, by rich and poor alike!

What is the fact? A few quotations from one of the most influential newspapers in the country may be taken as an introduction to this painfully-interesting subject of fœticide in the United States.

" Ladies' physician. Dr. A——, Professor of Midwifery; twenty-five years' practice; guarantees sure relief from whatever cause, with or without medicine; board and nursing."

"A truth. Mme. B——'s female medicines are warranted to remove all obstructions, from whatever cause, at one interview. Price, five dollars."

" Ladies' physician. Dr. C——, — Sumpter Place, guarantees immediate and pleasant relief to all unfortunates or no charge."

" Ladies risk their lives by improper treatment. Dr. D——, English Professor of Midwifery, removes irregularities, etc., without injury."

" Mrs. Dr. E——, — West 47th Street, female physician, guarantees relief from whatever cause. Board and nursing during confinement."

" Madame F——, Professor of Midwifery since 1850; office, No. — East Forty-seventh Street. Her Infallible Medicine No. 2, price, five dollars. Sold at druggists', — Grand Street, No. — Second Avenue; also, — Fulton Street, Brooklyn, or sent by mail."

The shamelessness of these advertisements has

no parallel in journalistic records. And it must be remembered that, although one New York paper in particular has acquired a disgraceful notoriety as the principal medium of these wholesale murderers, there are hundreds of other papers which admit notices, more or less direct, of the same nature, and that there is scarcely a city or large town throughout the length and breadth of the land but has its druggists' recommendations of Female Pills, Golden Remedies, etc., "warranted to remove all obstructions from whatever cause;" while reckless quacks make of the United States mail an agent to carry desolation and death into thousands of widely-scattered families through the dissemination of pamphlets bearing alluring titles, such as "The Private Medical Companion," "Secret Physiology," "Advice to the Married," etc.,—all of them written with outward decency and in apparent good faith, but all really devoted to the vile object of enriching their authors or proprietors through the sins and sufferings of their victims.

The law of demand and supply always balances itself. It is an undeniable fact that the supply in the United States of agents and materials for procuring abortion is immense. What are the causes that produce the equally immense demand ?

There is evidently no excess of population to tempt parents to make away with their offspring, either born or unborn ; nor is the desire of unmarried women to remove the proof of their shame a sufficient explanation of the frequency of the crime, since, on account of the absence of hindrances to early marriage, seduction is not so common as in older countries; moreover, the majority of infants thus sacrificed belong to married mothers.

Apparently, though not really, the principal cause of the loose views and unprincipled conduct of American women in this matter is the demoralization produced by the rapid increase of luxury in living, and the adoption of French ideas and customs by wealthy inhabitants of large cities and hosts of families from all parts of the country, who, in these later years, make frequent and prolonged tours in Europe, choosing Paris as their headquarters, and its vanities as their model of social manners. It is true that many girls and matrons are thus spoiled for the pursuits of a sincere and earnest life; it is true that many of these fashionable women are, and are resolved to be, criminal with regard to the subject under discussion; but many others, who belong to the same class, are able to keep within the line of obvious natural duties; while thousands who know nothing of French vices, and are not placed in circumstances of temptation as regards luxurious pleasures, fall victims in their quiet homes to the horrible attractions of a sin which, more than any other they could possibly commit, possesses the power of pitiless and enduring revenge upon both body and soul.

This being the fact, it must be that there are certain general causes which are able to affect the sex alike, though under a great variety of outward conditions. One of the most powerful causes is, the lack of sufficient physiological instruction in girlhood. Not only are the text-books expurgated, as far as possible, of the sexual idea, which, of course, they must be for the use of mixed schools and very young people, but mothers seldom talk seriously and freely with their growing daughters upon the vast importance and sacred ultimate design of the crisis that determines their maturity; and so girls are left to imbibe false ideas and a dangerous half-knowledge from the revelations of their more inquisitive mates, and allowed to sully the purity of their awakening feelings by speculations upon relations which belong to a later period of life, and which judicious mothers might easily persuade them to avoid thinking about until passion should have time to become tempered by mental training, and a more extended observation of the realities of human existence should prepare them to enter with becoming seriousness upon the duties and responsibilities which marriage involves. Hence, many girls at their maturity consider the periodical disturbance of their health as a transmitted "curse" from disobedient Eve, as a humiliating badge of their inferiority to the stronger sex, as a disagreeable hindrance to their work or their amusements, instead of as a provision which Nature is thus early and carefully making for the next generation; and if they do not recklessly squander their stock of health in the selfish pursuit of pleasure, at least they scarcely ever guard and develop their physical powers in order that, at some future time, they may be more fit to become mothers.

Another powerful source of subsequent temptation is the reserve and mystery which is observed in many American families towards all subjects relating to the union of the sexes. There is no people in the world so reticent in such matters as the Americans. The habit is probably a trace of the old Puritan influence, under whose sway the sweet human affections were only tolerated as a necessary evil, and their natural results accepted with a shamefacedness which might well depress young and inexperienced observers.

Every American, on first becoming familiar with the customs of Europeans, either through foreign travel or acquaintance with immigrants at home, must be struck by the ease and simplicity with which family details of pregnancies and births are mentioned by such persons. Not only is a supposed conception by a royal wife announced without delay by the newspapers, but women in less exalted stations receive ·the good wishes of their friends for an early fruition of their parental aspirations, and are congratulated as soon as tokens of their fruitfulness are evident. The general conviction that children are a blessing, and that there

is nothing to be ashamed of in acknowledging a
state of pregnancy, not only helps women to overcome the fears and depressions incident to that
condition, but is a great preservative against the
temptation to tamper with the processes of Nature
in cases where an addition to the family is, for
some reason, undesirable.

In America, women often avoid speaking of
their situation to their nearest relatives or most
intimate friends, and it is to be feared that in many
cases this reticence is preserved for the express
purpose of facilitating an abortion, should such a
termination be resolved upon.   But even when
no crime is meditated, the process is apt to go on
under the unwholesome shadow of a great silence :
the necessary wardrobe for the expected little
stranger is prepared in secret and kept under lock
and key; no allusion to the approaching event is
made on the part of neighbors and friends, and the
candidate for maternal honors is often so ashamed
of her altered form and countenance as to shun the
sight of acquaintances, and even to refrain from
taking necessary exercise, receiving the punishment of her disregard of the laws of health in the
agonies of a protracted labor, including, not unfre-
quently, the loss of her child.*

---

* The writer would here state, once for all, that in this article
any statement descriptive of manners and customs connected
with the subject is put forth with due acknowledgment of the
existence of numerous instances to the contrary of what is alleged.

In one instance, three sisters who had been married within a short time of each other met at their mother's house, after a separation of nearly a year. All three were pregnant, and it would naturally be supposed that they would have congratulated each other and exchanged hopes and plans for the future of their offspring. Nothing of the kind. Two of the brides were unable to conceal their condition on account of the delicate health induced thereby; the third, more robust than the others, kept her situation a profound secret, and only confided it to her mother just before her departure, with the proviso that her sisters should not be told.

Another lady, who had had a large family, concealed her latest pregnancy from her grown-up daughters and a maiden aunt who lived with her until concealment was no longer possible, and after that the fact was ignored by the whole circle. When her time arrived, the physician and nurse were summoned in all quietness, and neither

---

In thousands of American families sexual matters are considered with the true modesty of unembarrassed recognition, and pregnancy is welcomed, both by the prospective mother and her friends, with an intelligent regard to physical and moral laws; but it must be owned that there is a sufficient amount of ignorance and levity among women in general with regard to their peculiar function, to substantiate the writer's remarks, and to justify the adducing of the instances herein contained, every one of which is not only authentic, but stands as a representative of many others that might be given.

4

daughters nor sister were informed of what had
happened until, the next day, they were invited
into the chamber to greet the newly-arrived infant.

Why there should be such reserve in a matter
which is certain soon to advertise itself, it would
be hard to explain.   In some cases, the feminine
love of mystery seems to be the ruling motive; in
others, a false shame or an overweening fastidious-
ness and delicacy.

But, though such whims would seem to be an
individual matter, they are really of general interest, because their consequences are sometimes
highly injurious.   In two cases, at least, that have
come under the writer's observation, the whole life
of children born of mothers who were ashamed
of their pregnancy (the one because she was past
age, the other because she was mawkishly modest)
was rendered a burden to them through an unnatural and, at the same time, unconquerable shy-
ness and aversion to being seen by their fellows;
so that, although both of them were men of fine
physical health and good intellect,—possessed also
of education and wealth and station to assist them
in running a useful and honorable career,—all these
good gifts were rendered null by a pre-natal curse,
and neither they nor the world were the better or
the happier for their having been born.

In pleasant contrast with the above instances of
maternal selfishness and vanity, arises the picture
of a certain New England mother who, as the

time approached when another little one was to be
added to the flock, allowed her two daughters
(only eleven and thirteen years of age) to assist
her in making the wardrobe for the expected baby,
talking to them the while of what they must do
during her illness and in case of her death, and
leaving upon their young minds so pleasant an
impression of the fortitude and serenity with which
a woman can go forward towards her fate in that
strange crisis which involves so much of joy or
sorrow, that they were saved forever from any
temptation to shrink from the same destiny in
their own case.

Said a woman who has mourned for many years
the sin committed in her youth, "I can hardly
realize that it is I myself who perpetrated so unnatural a crime, my whole character, now that it
is developed, is so strangely imbued with the
maternal instinct. And, in looking back to try to
understand what it was that led me so far astray
from my duty, I cannot help thinking that my
temptation was founded, in great measure, upon
the unworthy ideas which, through my early
training, I had always connected with sexual
matters. For instance, at home I was taught to
call a bull a 'great animal,' and a cock a *rooster;*
and I remember to this day the reproachful glance
that I received from a matronly relative when I
once exclaimed, on seeing a flock of sheep go by,
'Oh, there is a ram!' As I grew older, I occa-

sionally heard from the elders of my own sex a
sarcastic remark concerning some woman who
ventured to walk in the streets when conspicu-
ously advanced in pregnancy, or some mother
who had added another infant to her already large
family of children; but never a word in confirma-
tion of the Psalmist's assertion that 'children and
the fruit of the womb are a heritage and gift that
cometh of the Lord;' never a suggestion that the
private relations of husband and wife, with their
natural results, are in themselves sacred and to
be held in honor. On the contrary, I considered
that every married pair of my acquaintance who
had surrounded themselves with an abundance of
'pledges,' were in some way more indelicate than
those who had few children, or none at all; and,
in my own case, although natural impulse was
sufficiently strong and healthy to convince me that
I had not sinned against modesty in marrying the
man I loved, still I shrank from the prospect of
showing to the world a living evidence of our
intimacy, and was ready to take advantage of the
very favorable circumstances in which I happened
then to be placed for destroying the life that had
just begun, before its tokens had become manifest
to those around me. It is needless to expatiate
upon the utter silliness of my opinions at that
time, or to suggest that I greatly exaggerated, if
I did not wholly mistake, the feelings of my early
guardians, who would never have dreamed of com-

mitting the sin which I ventured upon with so little hesitation; but my melancholy history shows the danger of presenting any but the highest principles and motives to the consideration of young and inexperienced minds, since it is impossible to calculate how far a powerful imagination, a strong will, and a fearless ignorance may lead their possessor to carry out an erroneous deduction, based upon false premises, into disastrous practice."

Said another: "I spent my early girlhood in a small private school, conducted by a family of maiden sisters, who frequently took occasion to lecture us upon the modesty and reserve necessary to be maintained in our conduct when we should become active members of society. Occasionally they even went so far as to allude to our possible destiny as wives; but I cannot remember that a word ever escaped them concerning that most responsible of all situations in which most of us were likely one day to be placed,—as mothers. They probably considered it unwise to suggest such a topic, but I have often thought that if they had only uttered some earnest appeal to us to be true to the highest instincts of our sex in the event of maternity being offered us, I, and perhaps others of our number, might have been saved from yielding to a temptation which they must have known was abroad in society at that time."

Said another: "Many married women are in the habit of speaking of pregnancy as though it were a condition for which men were more responsible than women. The 'Sairey Gamps' among nurses, too, are apt to warn young girls of the tyranny in store for them in this particular, and to condole with suffering patients by remarking that if husbands could only be obliged to give birth to every alternate child, there probably would not be more than two children in each family, etc. I well remember hearing a lady, for whose character I had justly the highest reverence, say, in reference to a delicate girl who had married very early, 'Poor thing, she is foolish to tie herself down so young to having children!' I suggested, from a feeling of curiosity to hear more on the mysterious subject, 'Perhaps she will not have children yet awhile.' And the answer was, 'She cannot help herself if her husband choose that she shall have them!' My instinct of self-preservation, and with it my pride, were aroused by this admission, and my conclusion was, as that of many a high-spirited girl would have been, '*I have a right to decide whether I will subject myself to the temporary torture and continual care involved in the birth and nurture of a child.*' And so, when the time came, I *did* decide—in the negative, to my life-long remorse, my only excuse being that my husband was equally desirous of avoiding the trouble and expense of offspring, and equally blind as to the question of right and wrong involved in the commission of the deed."

Another reason why maternity is avoided by so many newly-married American wives is, that previous to their marriage they have become tired of and disgusted with children, on account of the trouble they have had with their younger brothers and sisters. In no other country are children, from infancy to adult years, so constantly the companions of their parents and other grown-up members of the family as in America. The scarcity of servants and the simplicity of household arrangements in general compel mothers and elder daughters to keep the little ones under their own eyes; and though this constant oversight on the part of the persons most interested in the children's welfare is, in many respects, an excellent thing, its obvious disadvantages are increased tenfold by the prevailing lack of parental discipline; whereby the younger members of the flock are rendered tyrants, and their seniors are forced to become their slaves.

Who has not seen how a little girl chafes at being compelled to forego the sports of a summer afternoon, and to sit in a hushed and darkened chamber, keeping the flies off a sleeping baby, that the mother may pursue her work in another part of the house? Who does not know that the plays of half-grown children are often utterly spoiled by the enforced companionship of "toddling wee things," who, however charming in the right place and at the right time, are only marplots to those

whose nimble feet are, as yet, impatient of restraint? And a few years later, when the girl is
beginning to rehearse for herself the absorbing
drama of friendship and love, how provoking is it
that the pleasant gatherings of young men and
maidens in her home must be embarrassed by the
pert chattering or round-eyed watchfulness of some
inquisitive six-year old; how disheartening that
the twilight confidences with the favored youth
must be suddenly put an end to by a summons to
come and put to bed a restless urchin, who must
have stories told him till he fall asleep, and who
does not scruple to inform his impatient Schehere-
zade—with often prophetic truth—that he is going
to keep awake a great while! The hasty vow
made by many an exasperated maiden under such
circumstances, that if ever she be married she will
not be tied down by children, is not seldom remembered and acted upon when the temptation comes.
Said a judicious mother when lamenting on one
occasion the scarcity of help for both kitchen and
nursery, " I am resolved, at whatever inconveni-
ence, not to allow my elder daughters to become
slaves to my younger children. Their turn for such
troubles will come soon enough, and I do not want
to disgust them with maternal duties beforehand."

And now let us listen to the regretful complaint
of one whose early feelings were not so kindly
consulted, and whose future was shadowed by
the extreme form of the very evil which the wise

woman above referred to deprecated as a probable result of premature care.

"In my childhood," she says, "I was remarkable for an overflowing and unselfish affection for every living thing that was smaller and more helpless than myself; dogs, cats, chickens, birds, and all other household pets were the delight of my heart; and as for babies, I loved them to idolatry. And so it came to pass that not only were my services called for in season and out of season by all members of the family in behalf of the little ones of our own nursery, but my visits to neighbors and friends were made use of in the same way; while the children of any guests who might be staying with us were given over almost wholly to my loving and patient care.

"This distinction was rather a pleasure than a trouble to me so long as I remained myself a careless, playful child, but as years went on and my mind began to expand with a desire of knowledge, and I longed for silence and solitude in order to carry on the ponderings and questions of an active intellect and an earnest soul, I became impatient of the restraints which had so long bound me; I felt that I ought to be allowed more individual opportunity, instead of being identified so completely with the younger lives that were developing around me. But circumstances were too powerful for my resistance, and the only result of my struggle was, that I gradually lost, through my perceptible discontent, the reputation for amiability which I had hitherto enjoyed, and which had tempted others to impose an unjust share of their own responsibilities upon me. At last I became free through my marriage, but when, soon afterwards, the prospect of a nursery of my own dawned upon me, I turned away in utter weariness, and would none of its once so fascinating fatigues. I imagined that I hated children, and believed that the instincts of my early years had not sounded the real key-note of my character. Now, when I recall the tender love I used to feel for my dolls, and the still more exquisite enjoyment I formerly took in the contemplation and care of infants, I am wild with regret at my folly in rejecting the (alas! only once-proffered) gift of offspring. My only comfort is in the fact that my crime has not lost me my rare power of attracting the affection of dumb animals and speechless babes,—the dogs of strangers still turn gladly to meet my caressing hand, and I can always woo the cherished child from the arms of its doting mother."

In cases where the fruit of a first conception is prematurely destroyed, it is often through fear of the pains and perils of child-birth, which are erroneously supposed to be robbed of much of their intensity by being brought on at an early period of gestation. American women suffer more, probably, during parturition than the women of any other people. They are born into a climate which constantly stimulates the nervous system, and this physical sensitiveness reacts upon the mental forces, especially upon the imagination. Native delicacy of constitution is fostered by ambition in intellectual pursuits, by indulgence in fashionable follies, by enthusiasm in matters of religion; all of which excesses are due more to the goading effects of the climate than to any lack of equipoise in the national character.

It must be remembered, too, that Americans of the present day are suffering, not only from the wearing influences of an unprecedented excitement of affairs inseparable from the rapid growth of a prosperous republic, but from inherited weakness, resulting from the over-exertions of their progenitors, those notable grandmothers, who, stimulated by the necessity of individual labor in every department of social life in a newly-settled country, emulated each other in remaining at the wash-tub, or the cook-stove, or the spinning-wheel, until the pangs of maternity compelled them to desist for a time from their unyielding industry.

The children born out of all this hurry and worry were, in many instances, weak, fretful, morbid, and, succeeding to the same habits which had robbed themselves of their due share of vitality, gave to their descendants a still greater sensitiveness of nerves with a still more limited power of endurance; so that, by reason of these unfortunate pre-natal influences, and the debilitating effects of the climate, and the confusion of a rapidly-developing civilization, the majority of the women of America are weak, nervous, imaginative, withering with marvelous and pitiable celerity under the cares of marriage and maternity, and losing, through ill health and failure of spirits, not merely their own comfort and the admiration of society, but in many cases the affection of their husbands; who often show a strong perception of the contrast between the faded wife of a few years' possession and the fresh charms of her yet unwedded female friends.

What wonder, then, that many a wife, still too youthful to realize the beauty of that law of Nature which gives to mothers a second spring-time in their daughters' bloom, should seek to prolong the period of her own unrivaled dominion in the heart of the man she has chosen to be her constant and exclusive lover, and should be tempted to consider any means as lawful to so apparently laudable an end?

American girls marry too young; before they have learned to understand even their passional, still less their affectional and moral, nature. They mistake the first sexual inclination for that recognition of a kindred spirit which should alone determine the choice of a life-companion; and so, when the only partially developed baser instinct is prematurely satiated, there is often not enough affection and respect remaining for the partner of these fleeting physical joys to foster the desire that ought naturally to succeed,—to become the mother of his children.

Said a young girl, fresh from boarding-school, when relating to a friend of her own age an offer of marriage which she had just received and accepted, "The first thing I thought of was, what a horrid thing it would be to have a young one right off!" She married and *did* have, not only one "young one," but a series of them, and is now, though still in her twenties, a faded, worn-out woman, whose children show plainly that they have been defrauded of a large share of vitality, that is the birth-right of every human being.

Many a girl shrinks from marriage on account of the successive burdens that are likely to become her portion in that state ; and many a bride looks beyond the joys of the honeymoon to the distress that nine other moons will probably bring, and meditates in advance a speedy escape from their threatened terrors.

Said a woman who has never ceased to regret an early sin against her motherhood, " While I was debating the subject in my own mind,—being tempted to the crime chiefly through the fact that my sister had suffered extremely during child-birth, and the corresponding fear that I, who was even more slight and delicate than she, would surely lose my life in the struggle,—my mother-in-law—who had not yet overcome the natural jealousy caused by seeing another holding the first place in the affections of a favorite son—took occasion, one day, while talking with a neighbor, to expatiate with all the eloquence of truth upon the frightful agonies she had suffered during parturition; saying, by way of climax, that, old as she was, it made the cold sweat start at every pore only to recall that long-past experience. What possessed her to speak in this manner, suspecting, as I think she did, my situation at the time, I cannot imagine; at all events, in my then excitable state, her words were daggers to my heart, and I left the room fully resolved to take speedy measures to spare myself the full measure of the tortures I could not expect entirely to avoid."

Said another, whose childlessness is a matter of regret to all who know her well enough to recognize her remarkable capacity for influencing the young, "Just as I had reached an age when girls begin to dream that life is, or may be, all poetry and romance, I went to visit one of my mother's early friends, the idolized wife of a man much older than herself, and with no children to disturb the luxurious silence of her stately mansion. The change from the crowded nursery and noisy parlor of my own home was extremely agreeable, and the longer I stayed the more enviable appeared, to my inexperienced mind, the lot of my gay, untroubled hostess. Whether she secretly longed for offspring I cannot tell, but she frequently expressed her thankfulness that she had been spared maternal cares and anxieties, and especially that she had not been called upon to undergo the agonies of child-birth, of which she had such a morbid dread that her remarks filled me with an undefined terror, and I privately resolved never to allow myself to be brought to that extremity of suffering. Years afterward I married; and with the first symptoms of pregnancy arose in full force my memories of that happy, childless home, and, alas! with these came back also the frightful impressions of the hour of travail, allusions to which had formerly made my blood run cold. So I yielded to sudden temptation, and committed a deed which, I am convinced, the woman whose conversation had exerted so powerful an influence over my opinions would never have thought of attempting had the suffering she deprecated threatened to become a part of her own experience."

There is no doubt that the general tone of the fictitious literature of the present age—the novels, and magazine stories, and narrative poems, which young girls read with such avidity—has an indirect influence upon the spread and increase of this crime. The novels of a hundred years ago, though they seem coarse and immoral to the refined taste of to-day, treated the relation of the sexes in a point-blank manner, which at least left no doubt in the mind of the reader as to the matter-of-fact element in the passion of love.

In the famous story of " Pamela," for instance, the avowed object of the hero, from first to last, is the possession of the person of the heroine ; one of his earliest propositions is the offer of a suitable provision for the offspring that would be likely to result from the gratification of his licentious desires ; and even after the persistent virtue of Pamela has shamed him into respecting her maiden innocence and led him to offer her honorable marriage, it is still his undisguised longing for the delights of the nuptial bed which prompts him to urge for a speedy celebration of the prefatory religious rites.

The woes of Clarissa Harlowe, too, were all due to the permitted empire of the brute instinct over the noble qualities of her unprincipled lover ; and the fact that the pure-minded women of Richardson's time could read these books without disgust, nay, with enthusiastic admiration, is a proof that they considered excessive lust as a natural characteristic of the opposite sex, and beheld in themselves the Heaven-appointed ministers to the enjoyment of their lords and masters.

But with the gradual elevation of woman, novels have kept up a proportionate exaggeration of the real sentiment of society. When women began to write their own impressions of what love ought to be, the bed was kept out of sight, and only occasional chaste embraces testified to the slight admixture of an earthly element in the sublime devotion of the mutually-elected pair.   And so volumes were written in description of the ecstasies, the sorrows, the temporary misunderstandings, jealousies, and alienations of a virtuous courtship, extending often over a period of years, and culminating in a romantic marriage, with which event the story came to an end, and the interest of the reader also went no farther. Who cared whether children came to bless the home of a couple so entirely happy in each other? It is enough that he continued always the attentions of a lover, that she retained her place as the mistress of his affections and the heroine of his fondest fancies.

With women love is always more a sentiment than a passion, and this is especially true of young girls, who rarely experience any stronger sexual emotion than is contained in the undefined magnetism attaching to the presence of the other sex, or the confused pleasure felt on receiving a caress from the person beloved. Hence, women enjoy, and like to prolong, the suggestive period of courtship, and would fain extend its enchantments into the prosaic realities of married life. At best, they feel that their own love story came far behind the pathetic experiences of the Amandas and Melissas of their favorite novels ; nor are they willing to descend from their proud position as Orlando's idol and to gradually settle down into

"Something better than his dog, a little dearer than his horse."

* Least of all are they desirous of allowing a rival

5*

in his affection in the person of a child, who, while causing the ruin of the health and beauty of its mother, will almost certainly destroy the last illusion of romance by bringing care and trouble without end into the hitherto snug and quiet home.

Let the young wife preserve her slender form and blooming countenance to delight her husband's eye; let her retain her place on his knee, and charm him with her girlish gayety in the sweet moments of welcome that bring them together after the business of the day is over; or, when the excitement of society is sought as an agreeable change, let her be free to accompany him to opera and ball, awakening afresh his admiration by cunning devices of her toilette, and piquing him to new devotion through the attentions which other men are proud to pay her. Is not this better than to fade away in one brief year into the languid mother, worn out with watching over the cradle of a cross or sickly child, having no time to share her husband's leisure, and no energy to call up the sprightly sallies which had made her so fascinating in the free and happy days of her girlhood and before this helpless intruder came to spoil the perfection of their wedded bliss? This may be an unnatural way of thinking and feeling, but it is the way in which many a young mother *does* think and feel; and the temptation to rebel against her destiny is increased with every new drain upon her easily-exhausted vigor, especially if to the cares which belong to maternity be added the anxieties attendant upon a limited provision for the wants of an increasing family.

One would think that after a woman has once borne a child, she would realize the sacredness of life and the tenderness of the tie between a mother and her infant sufficiently to protect her forever from any temptation to betray her trust in this particular. But, alas! such is not always the result of maternal experience. Women become tired out with the duties of the nursery, angry at the rapid decay of their beauty and strength, discouraged at the expense which every new addition to the family creates, and so, as they are unable to save themselves by prevention, they try cure.

And here we strike upon another main reason for the prevalence of fœticide, as well as discover the woman's best excuse for its perpetration. It was recently asserted at an American meeting of a society for social improvement, that until woman obtains the control of her own person she will continue to outrage her nature by ridding herself of the children she is unwilling to bear. It is a fact that the majority of married women are slaves to excessive sexual passion in their husbands, and that any attempt on the part of the wife to assert her own rights in this respect is productive of so much domestic infelicity, that she submits and endures rather than see anger and sullenness added to selfishness and lust in her husband's character and conduct.

Excepting in rare and abnormal instances, the sexual desire in woman is weak, by reason of her training, compared to its degree in man, and is combined with so many other feelings,—during virginity with the sentiment of love, and after marriage with a consciousness of the responsibility attached to its probable consequences,—that if women had their own way in the matter this physical intercourse would take place at comparatively rare intervals, and only under the most favorable circumstances. Such an arrangement would be of infinite benefit to the race: men would preserve their vigor, and women their beauty and spirits, and though fewer children might be born, their quality would be improved. As the case stands, and has thus far always stood, the selfishness of men towards women meets with a heavy punishment in the early failure of the health of wives and the physical and mental shortcomings of offspring.

Indeed, in most cases, mothers cannot be said to entertain, in relation to their prospective honors, any stronger feeling than that of resignation; while many deplore openly the fate which, through principle or fear, they dare not tamper with, and entail upon their children the evil temper and morbid depression with which, during the moment-ous period of dual life, their own souls are filled. How many feel themselves at liberty to take revenge for their condition by indulging all the whims that a capricious fancy, stimulated by an empty mind, can devise! How many dress and dance and frolic with renewed zeal, in anticipation of the period of retirement that must follow, and resort to all cruel devices of the toilette to hide, as long as may be, the increasing alterations in face and form! How few are they who, during the period of gestation, train body and soul, not only or mainly with a view to their own health and comfort, but principally for the sake of the invisible being who is receiving every instant impressions which will expand later into its individual capacity and character!

Another temptation peculiar to American society is the almost total absence of supervision and interference on the part of the government in domestic concerns. In older countries, where every change of residence must be immediately communicated to the police, where no powerful medicine is sold by the apothecaries without an order from a physician, where every birth must be recorded by special authorities, and every death certified to by a doctor, there is slight chance to tamper with a deed of darkness which requires time and secrecy for its perpetration. It is only in the United States that such advertisements as have been quoted could be published with impunity in the newspapers, as it is only here that suspected or well-authenticated instances of fœticide could take place

unchallenged by the civil authorities and ignored
by public opinion. For the momentary excitement
occasionally roused by the discovery of a criminal
of this sort among the lower classes, or a faint
attempt to make an example of some unlucky
quack who has been seized upon as a scape-goat
for his more prosperous brethren in wickedness,
cannot be considered as any proof of an earnest
determination on the part of the American people
to punish the guilty and protect the weak in all
that concerns this dreadful evil.

One safeguard to the sanctity of the family
which exists in aristocratic countries is wanting,
or, at most, has but a feeble influence, in America:
namely, the desire of perpetuating the rank and
estates of a powerful race or the glories of an
honored name. One can easily understand the
anxiety which a reigning queen or the wife of an
heir-apparent to the throne must feel, lest through
her unfruitfulness the crown should pass from that
branch of the royal family to which she belongs;
and the same responsibility, in some degree, rests
upon all who are chosen by great hereditary lords
to enjoy and hand down the splendors of their
ancestral halls. One of the most pathetic bits of
court gossip ever chronicled is the account of a
dangerous illness of Catharine of Braganza, wife
of Charles the Second, who, after having longed
for years for an heir, betrayed the secret grief of
her heart by raving constantly in her delirium of

the imaginary boy she had given the king, complaining that it was "an ugly boy;" while the "merry monarch," amiable even in his disappointment, tried to pacify her by repeating, " Nay, Kate, it is a very pretty boy!" And who that pores over the domestic history of all countries, the books of heraldry, the records of the peerage, the inscriptions upon tombstones, but recognizes somewhat of the disappointment involved in the final statement, " died without issue," and guesses that in many a coat of arms the presence of a " bar sinister" would be less a matter of regret than the absence of an " escutcheon of pretense"?

But in America—where property cannot be entailed, where it is seldom the case that a family inhabits the same house, or even dwells in the same vicinity, for more than one generation, and where the majority of married couples go out into a new region to build up gradually for themselves a home and a fortune—this feeling of responsibility towards both the past and the future is naturally weakened, and the overworked wife is in danger of being led to believe that her own comfort is the chief object to be consulted in the question of the acceptance or rejection of maternity. And yet no guardianship by government is so sure a preventive of wrong as is the check of an intelligent conscience, and no title of nobility was ever so worthy of being preserved and handed down as is the citizenship of a free Republic!

The query naturally arises here, Do not women know that they are doing wrong when they intentionally destroy the fruit of the womb? Yes, they know it, just as men know that they are doing wrong in visiting brothels, in getting drunk, in cheating and lying, and indulging bad tempers. And yet, not so clearly as these latter. The sins of licentiousness, intemperance, and anger consist in the excessive indulgence of a natural impulse; fœticide is a crime against nature, and therefore its character is not rightly understood before its committal, while the remorse that follows is proportionately severe and unappeasable.

All right-minded men are justly filled with horror at the thought of this cruel practice. But right-minded women, however entirely they may condemn the deed, have yet a sufficient comprehension of the temptations that lead to it to pity, even more than they blame, those of their sisters who thus risk the health of both body and soul in a vain attempt to escape the destiny of their sex.

Said one of these victims of early ignorance, " During the first years of my repentance, when I was almost insane with unavailing sorrow, I became acquainted with one of the purest and loveliest specimens of my own sex that I have ever known. From the first she manifested a preference for my society, and soon showed a disposition to select me as a confidential friend. But this distinction I felt myself unworthy to accept, and I finally re-

K

solved to confess the secret to her and be guided, concerning my future estimate of myself, by her judgment as to my sin. She listened to the story with surprise and pity, but without any signs of aversion, and, in trying to lighten my evident despair, she begged me to consider the fact as a mistake ; sad and eventful certainly, but by no means indicative of my real character, nor decisive as to its power to blast my future career. This true woman, true wife, true mother, true friend, saved me. from myself at a terrible crisis, and her unabated confidence and affection have since been as a strong shield against the keen darts of remorse which, ever and anon, have threatened to overcome my courage."

When one considers who the majority of the persons are that commit this crime, one is convinced that there is some influence at work stronger than any that has been cited, which, in combination with ordinary temptations, is able to lead a tender-hearted and generally conscientious woman so far out of the way of her duty. One can understand how savages may override their gentler instincts, until infanticide has become a lauded custom or even a religious rite ; how the ignorant populace of overcrowded heathen countries may be prompted to take the simplest means of checking the surplus demand for food ; how here and there in Christian lands a well-born maiden, who has been betrayed by her lover, or an unbefriended servant-girl, who finds it hard enough to work for her own support, should make away with a token of shame and a future encumbrance; but how it is that married women, educated, refined, modest, and moral in every other respect, loving the children they have allowed to be born with devoted affection, and mourning those who have died a natural death with a grief like that of " Rachel,"— how such as these can ever allow any circumstance of life to blind them to the iniquity of the crime of fœticide, is a mystery that demands long searching for its solution.

May not the key to this riddle be found in the general belief in the forgiveness of sins through the atonement of Jesus Christ? This is a startling suggestion; but any one who has made a study of the subject must acknowledge that there is some ground for the idea.

Probably all persons who have watched closely the workings of the human heart—either through their own conflicts with temptation or through the revelations of other remorseful souls—have noticed that what lent security to doubt before the committal of a sin, as well as gave keener poignancy to after-regret, was the thought, " *If I find that I have done wrong, I can repent, and Jesus Christ will forgive me!*"

The apparent insincerity of this argument is removed when one remembers how the real nature of evil is hidden, or rather, transfigured, through the presence of temptation. The qualities of vice, as well as of virtue, are relative rather than abstract, and it is easy to find sufficient excuses for what one wishes earnestly to do. So when a woman would fain prevent the approaching sufferings and cares of maternity, she bethinks herself of circumstances that would suffice for the justification of an act which she is trying to reason herself into considering as unimportant, but which Nature is all the while hinting to be momentous. Her husband is poor, and ought not to be burdened with a family until his business becomes established; she herself is delicate, and would probably die in child-bed, leaving her infant to the miseries of orphanage; the child would be likely to inherit her weaknesses and diseases, and what merit is there in conferring life without bestowing health to make it enjoyable? The anxieties caused by insufficient means, and by her unwillingness to become a mother, must react unfavorably upon the disposition of the child; very likely it would be an idiot, or hopelessly perverted in temper; perhaps, after all, these physical symptoms are not caused by pregnancy; surely there is no harm in resorting to remedies to restore the normal condition of health; or, should the unwelcome suspicion be true, there is, as yet, no "life" in the embryo, and so the strictest moralist could not call its intentional destruction murder. Finally, if all that has been written and spoken in favor of a woman's right to determine whether she will become a mother or not be a false doctrine, and she really be not at liberty to refuse to bear the consequences of having yielded to the instinct of love, then her doubt and ignorance will be taken into consideration at the judgment, and whatever degree of sinfulness was comprised in her act will be forgiven and blotted out by a merciful Saviour.

This perversion of faith, this cowardly and ungrateful wounding of Christ afresh in the house of his friends, this determination to "sin that grace may abound," is only another form of the more common and patent iniquity which prevails among all peoples, whether pagan or Christian, where religion is divorced from morality through a general belief in an atonement for sin, whether by sacrifices or by a sacrifice. It is the same inconsistency which leads "Christian statesmen" to plunder the national treasury and throw hindrances in the way of national purification, which makes pious monopolists defraud the community, and pious merchants, great and small, adulterate, and curtail, and falsify in disposing of their wares ; to say nothing of individual sins and shortcomings, whose influence is more directly seen by the offender.

If any one doubt that self-deception on this point has much to do with the frequent perpetration of the "nameless crime" among women, let such a one look about him, and see who and what manner of persons these are who thus revolt from their most obvious duty. Let him examine the note-books of honest physicians, who are so often shocked by confessions of evil-doing from patients whose whole character suggests nothing but what is lovely and of good report. The very fact that many women purposely exhaust their strength, in the hope of bringing on an abortion, by taking long country walks and climbing rugged moun-tains,—thus trying to perpetrate an unnatural crime in the very lap and bosom of Nature,—nay, that they will, with the same intent, painfully ascend to the top of a church spire,—perhaps of the very church in which they were married, and which stands ready to receive their children by baptism, —is proof sufficient that conscience is sometimes blinded through the flatteries of faith.

There is no other way of accounting for the inconsistency of such conduct. Many of the women who commit abortion are members " in good and regular standing" of a Christian church; many of them go from the table of the Lord to the couch of premature and induced labor, and present themselves again among the chosen flock of com-municants as soon as their health is sufficiently restored from the self-wrought injury. Almost all of these secret criminals are attendants upon Divine Service, and believers, more or less enthu-siastic, in the fundamental doctrines of orthodox Christianity. Nay, the case is not utterly unknown of a clergyman's wife yielding to the same sin;

and clergymen's wives are certainly often cognizant of the ravages of the crime in the congregations, however ignorant their husbands may be of its existence.

Said one of these matrons to a visitor who had inquired concerning the welfare of a mutual acquaintance belonging to the parish: "She would probably be a good deal healthier if she did not get rid of so many children!"

Said another, in speaking of a certain young lady who had brought distress upon her family by giving birth to an illegitimate child: "Why did not the foolish girl confess her situation earlier, so that her mother could have taken her to a doctor in New York and had the affair quietly done away with?"

The revelations also of remorseful victims substantiate this idea. Said a woman in whose character religious devotion was a prominent trait: "I must say this in my defense, that previously to committing the deed I did not consider it as an offense against God. My childish belief that each infant is a gift to its parents from heaven had faded before my later knowledge concerning the mystery of birth, and the theory of various apparently authoritative treatises that women have a right to limit the number of their offspring, together with the opinion prevalent among my sex that the fœtus has no life until it has quickened, rendered me insensible to the real nature of my act. My

illness—which I had calculated would be only a
short and slight interruption to a busy career of
church duties (considered by me at that period as
better for my own soul and more useful to my
fellow-mortals than would be the fulfilling of my
maternal functions)—was dangerous and protracted, but during its weary hours I felt no mis-
givings as to my culpability in having brought it
upon myself. When awake and rational, my mind
was full of the good I would accomplish on my
recovery; and the intervals of delirium were made
happy by the fancy that Jesus was keeping watch
at the foot of my bed and regarding me with looks
of favor, in pledge of his acceptance of my earnest
service. It was not until I had resumed my chosen
work that I gradually learned the value of the
privilege I had rejected; and then even harder to
bear than the yearnings of my unsatisfied mother-
love was the thought that I had robbed the Master
I adored of one of his 'jewels;' that through my
instrumentality one soul would be wanting to his
triumph as Redeemer, one voice lacking in the
chorus of praise to 'the Lamb that was slain!'"

It is often brought forward as an argument in
favor of the Catholic Church that fœticide is never
committed by its members. But this assertion is
unwarranted. France, to which all other nations
owe the greatest pressure of influence tending to,
as well as the most skillful appliances for, the perpetration of this crime, is a Catholic country; and

in Paris the majority of those who commit this, among other sins, are actual members of the Catholic Church. In Italy, the very nest and fountain-head of Catholicism, the women, especially of the higher classes, do all in their power to prevent pregnancy, and many of them do not hesitate to put a premature end to its development when it does occur. Here, too, priests as well as laity are involved in the universal scandal; and infanticide, if not fœticide, is so generally believed to be a frequent element in the secret experience of the cloister, that the charge would seem to be not wholly founded upon the prejudiced suspicions of members of a hostile faith. In Germany, both of these crimes occur frequently among the unmarried women of the lower classes in Catholic cities; and it is the terrors of the civil, rather than the restraints of the ecclesiastical, law that prevent a still greater waste of fœtal and infantile life. In the Cathedral of Augsburg may be seen to-day in the confessionals a printed notice, informing penitents that for the crimes of perjury, violence to parents, voluntary and unjustifiable homicide, incendiarism, and *abortion, whether produced by instruments or by drugs, and whether the fœtus be born alive or dead*, the penance is to be determined by the Ordinarius.

There is no doubt that Catholic priests in America are vigilant and strict in trying to prevent the commission of fœticide among their parishioners.

The frankly-avowed object of the Romish Church is to obtain religious and political supremacy through the only means possible in a Republic,—the possession of a majority of the citizens. With this end in view the Church is laboring with indefatigable zeal to increase her numbers through immigration, conversion, adoption, and the natural increase of families already under its control.

It may be well now to inquire what part men play in this secret tragedy of household crime. There are, probably, few instances of women committing fœticide where the men most concerned are not at least consenting unto the premature death ; and occasionally we read in criminal trials repulsive accounts of husbands or lovers urging, and even commanding, their partners to commit the deed. It happens sometimes, however, that wives and mistresses destroy the fruit of their bodies in secret, knowing well that the mere suggestion of such an act would meet with a horrified protest and refusal. But thousands of husbands, who would not hear of putting an end to embryonic life already begun, resort continually on their own part to various precautions against the natural results of cohabitation, and encourage their wives to practice a similar foresight. Now, there is not so wide a difference as at first appears between thwarting the designs of Nature in the outset and interrupting her processes after they are fairly commenced, and there is no doubt that fœticide is made easy to many a conscience through an habitual nullification of the sexual act.

Physicians too, in general, are by no means entirely innocent of the murder of unborn children. Not to speak of professed abortionists and reckless quacks, is it not true that in every large city and populous country district of the United States certain doctors, otherwise honest in practice and thoroughly upright in their social relations, are singled out by common report as "willing to help women out of their troubles"? Do not many physicians, conscious that great sexual wrongs are practiced under the protection of marriage, and moved to pity by the complaints of women worn out by too frequent child-bearing, consent to "remove obstructions," trusting in their professional skill to prevent injurious consequences? And even when a proposal of this kind is met by the medical adviser with a prompt refusal, does he do all in his power to avert the catastrophe, by enlightening the patient as to the true nature of the contemplated act and its probable effect upon her physical and moral well-being?

Take the following true story as an instance in point:

A certain physician was summoned to a confidential interview with a married pair, in whose family he had practiced for a considerable time. The woman was pregnant, and both she and her husband were desirous that the encumbrance should be done away with. The case was a peculiar one. The woman had already given birth to many children; but, though apparently healthy herself, her infants had all been feeble, and only two had survived the first year; while frequent miscarriages had occurred during the intervals between the regular births. Indeed, pregnancy in her case might be regarded almost in the light of a chronic disease; and at last, wearied with the constant drain upon her physical energies, as well as disheartened by the grievous experience of seeing the untimely withering of so many precious buds of hope, she decided to resort to artificial means of destroying the foetus, in the hope of thereby arresting the excessive tendency to conception.

The physician, to whom all the circumstances were familiar, consented to prepare a medicine for the purpose, warning the woman, however, that should she ever again become pregnant she would probably die at the birth of the child. She took the potion, and the wished-for result occurred. But her constitution resisted even this shock, and in a few months she was again pregnant. As soon as she discovered her situation her health began to decline, whether from the effects of the physician's poison or of his prophecy can never be known; she fell into a morbid melancholy, and died before her term was accomplished, the child dying with her.

Now, here is a case where all parties acted openly, and, in a certain sense, honorably. There was no deception towards any person interested in the event, and no apparent realization of the moral guilt incurred; the physician was a regular practitioner, and the married couple were persons of respectability and good position. Yet the error involved the sacrifice of three lives, to say nothing of the burden of responsibility that, one would think, must forever weigh down the consciences of the surviving participators in the deed.

The enormity of the crime of fœticide may be, in some degree, estimated by the excessive remorse which, sooner or later, is sure to follow its perpetration. Probably the willful taking of human life, though not under all circumstances the greatest of crimes, must ever appear such in the retrospection of him who commits it. There is something positive and palpable in the shedding of blood, from which sense, as well as sentiment, revolts. The shaft of slander may strike as surely and with keener pain than the pistol-shot or the dagger; but the wound is secret and its working slow, and the enemy comforts himself with the belief that the blasted life or the untimely death is not wholly or mainly of his causing. The man who betrays the innocence of a young girl feels less self-reproach on account of the gradual death of her soul in a subsequent career of vice, than he would experience if she were to end at once her shame and despair by suicide. It was the "damned spot," "the smell of blood," that not all the perfumes of Arabia might sweeten, upon Lady Macbeth's hand, that maddened her; if the same hand had only signed away the life of Duncan, her remorse would not have been so violent.

If, then, the remembrance of murder committed through anger, or envy, or greed of gold, or any other bad passion concentrated for the moment upon the victim, be so bitter, and the blood of a stranger or an enemy have such power to haunt, think what must be the anguish of a mother who deliberately wastes the sources which supply at once strength to herself and existence to her unborn child, and sees before her eyes the unfinished wreck of a being whom, a few months later, she would have pressed to her bosom with a tenderness which no other object has power to awaken! It is well known that grief for the loss of an infant at birth is always a great drawback to a woman's recovery from confinement, and is frequently the cause of her death; how much more terrible, then, must be the blank in her outlook upon the future, when the weary hours of pain and weakness are burdened with the uneasy doubts of a wider experience or the keen pangs of a speedily-awakened remorse!

Said one whose uncommon delicacy of feeling makes it exceedingly difficult to conceive of her ever having sinned against her organization in any manner: "If I had known beforehand anything of the awful processes of childbirth, I should have been effectually deterred from venturing to invoke them prematurely. I expected only a slight variation of the periodical disturbance which any woman, by a proper degree of care and cleanliness, is able to endure without great discomfort or aversion; and more dreadful to bear than even my agonizing suffering, were my fright and horror when I learned the extent of the catastrophe I had brought about. Let all inexperienced women know that there is not a more solemn scene on earth than the chamber of delivery; and she who is called to occupy that couch of pain needs, even more than natural strength or skillful attendance, the sustaining comfort of a good conscience, in the recollection that the gradual evolutions of Nature, and not the mischiefs of a devilish craft, have appointed the hour of travail!"

Said another: "It would almost seem that this crime, like many another, has its seasons of malignant prevalence; just as diseases, after having long existed in a sporadic form, now and then become epidemic. At the time when I fell a victim to the temptation, I was living in a country place, where all the newly-married women of the neighborhood were discussing the ideas derived from certain pamphlets of the 'Medical Companion' order, that had recently been circulated in that region. These women were unanimous in desiring to postpone pregnancy; and I have reason to think that several besides myself took measures to stop its progress after it had begun. But the generally-accepted opinion that we had a right to be the arbiters of our own destiny in this particular, prevented any loss of self-respect on the part of the offenders, as well as of any position in society to which we were otherwise entitled; and it was not until after I had taken up my residence in a city, and through wider knowledge of the world had learned the true relation of the individual to the aggregate of humanity, that I recognized my real condition as a criminal, none the less because undetected and unpunished. And ever since, the thought that I have done something which has rendered me amenable to the law of every civilized country brings the blush of shame to my cheek, and serves as an effectual damper upon whatever degree of pride or satisfaction I might otherwise feel in the more praiseworthy deeds of my career."

Again, a retrospection of the crime of fœticide contains one element of self-torture which does not enter so largely into the remorse consequent upon the murder of beings already in existence. This element is a suggestion of the great happiness or widespread good which that prematurely-blasted life might have been able to confer upon its own generation and, perhaps, upon the whole race forever. Logically speaking, no event could happen otherwise than it does happen; since each

act of each individual is determined by his previous acts, and by the acts of all individuals that
have preceded him: but Regret scorns logic, and
continues its unavailing lament over what " might
have been."

Said a woman who, after many years of despond-
ency, had begun to realize the truth of Madame
de Staël's vigorous maxim,—*"Repeated penitence
wearies the soul,—it is a sentiment that can but once
regenerate us,"*—and to feel that atonement could
best be made through diligent and useful endeavor,—" From the moment when I began to
appreciate my irreparable loss, my thoughts were
filled with imaginings as to what might have
been the worth of that child's individuality; and,
especially, after sufficient time had elapsed to have
brought him to maturity, did I busy myself with
picturing the responsible posts he might have
filled, the honors he might have won, the joy and
comfort he might have brought to his suffering
fellow-creatures; nor, during the interval, have I
ever read of an accident by land or by water, or
of a critical moment in a battle, or of a good
cause lost through lack of a brave defender, but
my heart has whispered, ' *He* might have been there
to help and save ; *he* might have been able to lead
that forlorn hope ; *his* word or *his* deed might have
brought that wise plan to successful issue !' "

Said another : " I have often grown cold at the
thought—what if Mary, in despair at the misin-

terpretation of her character which her condition
would probably cause in the minds of all her
acquaintances, and especially in the mind of her
betrothed husband, had done violence to 'that
Holy Thing' which she carried beneath her heart!
I know I speak of an impossibility, and perhaps the
idea is blasphemous, but it has often occurred to
me that if every tempted woman would only look
at the matter from this stand-point, it would make
her afraid to destroy what might also become, in
an infinitely smaller degree, a savior of mankind!"

The same idea is suggested by one of the
most influential preachers of the present day, in a
familiar essay on the practical duties of life. After
several more remote allusions to the "nameless
crime," he says: "There is a word to say about
it that goes deeper than that of the physician, the
political economist, or the patriot. It is this: that,
in some way we cannot even imagine, we have
made the whole world poorer by what we have
done. What a loss to the world if once such a
sin had been hidden away in Stratford-upon-Avon;
or in the poor clay biggin two miles from Ayr, in
Scotland; or in the hut eight miles from Newcastle,
in England; or in many another place, shielded
and shrouded then as our homes are now, but
since then lifted up among the shining points of
the world! I could wish no worse hell for my
worst enemy, if I should ever take to bad wishing,
than that one should haunt him in eternity who

7*

might have come and poured mighty treasure into the common wealth of the world but for that sin!"

Thus finely and delicately can a tender-hearted man express his appreciation of this secret sin; but women know that it is not necessary to wait for eternity to be haunted by "one who might have come!"

A lady writer upon medical subjects, who has had a wide practical experience in the care of chronic female diseases, says, in reference to the agency of intentional abortion and its attendant remorse in causing nervous maladies: "There is a peculiar look in the eye, which I note, and dread the confession of such patients when they come for consultation."

Said one: "I think I was for a long time as near being insane as one can be without really going mad. Although much debilitated through the physical consequences of my sin, I often took long walks, much longer than I could have borne in health; and though going at a rapid pace, and without any pause for rest, I was as unconscious of fatigue as unimpressed by the features of the landscape, or by the persons and objects that I passed. I had an idea that I had lost, through that unnatural deed, the normal powers and qualities of a human being. I no longer ate and drank with the old hunger and thirst, nor slept the quiet sleep of innocence; I took no heed of the passage of time, and all that I saw and heard seemed to be the occurrences of a dream, as though life were already finished for me and I was observing it from another state of existence. The first ray of hope that dawned upon me was when, during an illness succeeding to this dangerous excitement, I found that the remedies prescribed for my feverish restlessness and excruciating headache affected me as they would have affected another person. From the moment of that discovery I began to amend in health, and have since recovered sufficient energy to interest myself in the work that seems to belong to me especially to do, though the strange feeling of having set myself apart from the rest of my sex, through that sin against my motherhood, will probably always remain to increase the bitterness of my childless and lonely condition."

Said another: "I envy a mother who goes to weep beside her baby's grave; because she knows where it is laid, and remembers how it looked in life, and is not ashamed to say, ' *I have lost a child.*' And when I hear mothers lamenting over such a loss, I pity them indeed; but I feel like saying to them, 'You think you are deeply afflicted, but your trouble is really light, because it is not mingled with remorse, and you are not to blame for the infant's death.' Truly, all sorrow that I have ever known or heard of is not to be compared with my sorrow, and that of others who have sinned in like manner!"

Another says: "I go to church in my despair,
and I hear the minister proclaim free pardon to all
sinners through the blood of Christ. Does he
know what he is saying? Would he offer me the
same comfort if he knew the extent of my guilt;
if he knew that I had sinned, presuming upon that
very grace which he declared is able to save to the
uttermost? And yet, if there be any truth in the
doctrine, it ought to apply to all kinds and degrees
of wickedness. But what avails God's forgiveness
if I cannot forgive myself? And what is salvation? Can God heal my self-inflicted wound, and
save me from the inevitable result of my evil
conduct? Nothing but a child can satisfy the
yearnings of maternal love; and I know of no
joys of heaven that could make me happy there,
unless this craving of my nature be first supplied
or the instinct annihilated. Somebody else may
have my crown and harp—*I want my baby!*"

Said another, whose strong intellect has led her
to philosophize as deeply upon the nature of her
sin as her warm heart has made her feel the bitterness of its consequences: "The only consolation
that I have been able to find is in the theory that,
through the remorse and punishment which attend
upon our faults and errors and sins, even more,
perhaps, than through the successful cultivation
of our virtues and good tendencies, is to be found
the necessary education of our souls."

This idea is sure to become a conviction in every

unprejudiced mind that has attained to a mature experience, having lent itself the while to a keen observation of the career of contemporaries and to a thoughtful review of the history of mankind.

David's height of spiritual purity was reached from the depths of adultery and murder; the wise piety of St. Augustine's manhood was the antithesis of his licentious youth; and Bunyan's Pilgrim groaned under the burden of the author's tainted memories.

Indeed, there is no record of any sincere and earnest life that does not reveal some soul-searching experience of grief or repentance as the root and main impulse of the after-development. There are characters, it is true, which do not appear to require the ploughing and harrowing of a great trouble, and to such the needed discipline is afforded by the ordinary changes, losses, and bereavements of this mortal life; but in others the soil must be prepared through a terrific shock. The wine made upon the slopes of Vesuvius is not better than much that is the product of smiling villages in other parts of the world, but it is famous because it is the late fruit of a once barren and blasted region; and so, in remembrance of the blackness of desolation from which luxuriance and strength have been redeemed, this blood of the grape receives the precious title of " Lachrymæ Christi" (*Christ's tears*).

" I can see," continues this sorrowful woman,

"that I have improved in many particulars through the influence of this trouble, and perhaps it was the only way to reach and eradicate certain faults in my character. But how do I know that I might not otherwise have been trained in a less severe school? and who am I that I must be bettered through another's loss? What good that I may be able to accomplish can ever atone to that infant's soul for its failure to obtain incarnation?"

These mournful revelations of remorse may fitly be concluded with the following extracts from records of an older time:

"In the 'Lives of the Saints' there is a curious legend of a man who, being desirous of ascertaining the condition of a child before birth, slew a pregnant woman; committing thereby a double murder, that of the mother and of the child in her womb. Stung by remorse, the murderer fled to the desert, and passed the remainder of his life in constant penance and prayer. At last, after many years, the voice of God told him that he had been forgiven the murder of the woman. But yet his end was a clouded one. He never could obtain an assurance that he had been forgiven the death of the child."—*Lecky, History of Morals*, ii. 26.

And here is the ancient Persian idea of the retribution that awaits this crime in another state of existence: "Then I saw the soul of a woman who ever dug an iron hill with her breasts; and an infant cried from that side of the hill, and the cry ever continued; but the infant comes not to the mother, nor the mother to the infant. And I asked thus: What sin was committed by this body, whose soul suffers so severe a punishment? Srôsh the pious, and Atarô the angel, said thus: 'This is the soul of that wicked woman who in the world became pregnant, . . . and she said thus: "I have not been pregnant." She also destroyed the infant.' I also saw the soul of a woman who ever came and went crying and wailing; upon her head, also, ever came pelting hail; and underfoot hot, molten brass ever streamed; and she ever gashed her own head and face with a knife. And I asked thus: What sin was committed by this body, that the soul ever suffers so severe a punishment? Srôsh the pious, and Atarô the angel, said thus: 'This is the soul of that wicked woman who became pregnant, . . . and she effected the destruction of the infant. Because of the pain and punishment, she fancies that she hears the cry of that infant, and she runs; and such vehemence of running is occasioned, as of one who walks upon hot brass; and she ever hears the cry of that infant, and gashes her own head and face with a knife, and demands the child; but she sees it not till the re-establishment of the world; this punishment she must suffer.' "—*The Book of Arda Viraf.*

THE ABUSE OF MATERNITY.

PART II.

THROUGH ITS UNWISE ACCEPTANCE.

" Man might by selection do something not only for the bodily
constitution and form of his offspring, but for their intellectual
and moral qualities.

"Both sexes ought to refrain from marriage if in any marked
degree inferior in body or mind; but such hopes are Utopian, and
will never be even partially realized until the laws of inheritance
are thoroughly known. All do good service who aid towards this
end." DARWIN.

S 77

PART II.

THERE are many ways of abusing maternity without resorting to pre-natal murder.

Any person who observes intelligently the over-crowded population of the Old World, cannot resist the conviction that there is a wise law of Nature which bids the human race restrain propagation as well as one commanding it to increase and multiply. The most hopeful philanthropy is struck dumb before the haggard multitudes of the London purlieus, and turns contemptuously from the incurable animalism of the swarming populaces of tropical climes. The world is becoming fuller every day. What is to be done when its whole surface is taxed to the utmost to support the existing generation; when industry has no further resources and invention no fulcrum for development? Such a period is sure to come if the present rate of increase be continued.

But without troubling ourselves concerning so remote a contingency, it is always true that every excess of population over the supply of food results, primarily, in the physical and moral degeneracy of

7

those who suffer from privation ; and, secondarily, in famines, wars, and pestilences which hurt and hinder all classes of society.

We are apt, in looking out upon the world, to imagine it as having been, for an indefinitely long period, in about the same condition as it is at present with regard to the number and situation of its inhabitants. But the smallest degree of reflection convinces us of our mistake. Without discussing the question as to whether man was " made" or " evolved," we know that the existence of the species has been, in comparison with that of the natural elements, of short duration. All the nations of which we have any knowledge can be traced to their beginnings ; nor is there anything in the occasionally-discovered relics of pre-historic man to imply that the race was ever before so numerous or so wide-spread as it has now become.

Its increase, too, is constantly cumulative. Not only is human life less exposed than formerly to destruction from the ravages of wild beasts and from a general state of lawlessness among men, but its average length is actually greater, by reason of improvements in domestic habits, in cooking, ventilation, and drainage ; nor can we set a limit to the possibility of gain in this particular. The devastations of famine are now, in a great measure, prevented by the timely aid which modern methods of conveyance enable more favored regions to ex- tend to places threatened by want ; the virulence of pestilence is greatly subdued by progress in pathological science, and epidemics of all kinds will eventually be rooted out by universal cleanliness. War, the most artificial mode of reducing population, will cease before long to be the final arbitrator of national differences. Not only is the moral sense of every civilized people more and more opposed to its barbarous incidents, but no country can bear much longer the drain of expense attendant upon keeping a large body of its citizens inactive in times of peace, nor the waste of so much of its best blood by the terrible modern engines of battle.

So, then, we see that the former principal checks to over-population are fast being removed through the progress of knowledge, while the resources of the earth are continually becoming more limited by man's encroachment upon its space. Fields and forests are everywhere being covered with houses and manufactories. Cattle, which furnish milk and meat, are penned up in narrow boundaries until they breed disease to their own destruction and that of their human consumers. Already the hungry millions of Europe are turning for food to the herds that have heretofore roamed unmolested the immense plains of the Western Continent and the islands of the Southern seas, and only a comparatively small portion of the fertile surface of the earth is still virgin to the plough and the grain-drill. Moreover, the invention of machinery for all kinds of labor is continually lessening the demand for human agents; and, though the opening of many new regions to emigration has thus far prevented the difference being felt, there will come a time when this resource for superfluous bone and sinew will not exist.

It is no weakening of the argument to assert that there are, as yet, food, and space, and work enough in the world for all of its inhabitants; since it is a fact that the race is constantly increasing, while the necessary supplies for its subsistence are steadily diminishing. Indeed, even now the majority of human beings are not able to obtain either a sufficient quantity or a proper quality of food for their healthy physical development; while a great proportion of those who succeed in securing a decent support are obliged to spend all their time and powers in its acquirement, to the neglect of their intellectual growth. So long as this is true, the race cannot be said to have attained to a condition favorable to the exertion of its highest capacities.

But the fault is not wholly in excess of numbers; it lies also in the inferior quality of individuals. Who, in looking upon the mass of his contemporaries, can say that he is proud of his species? nay, what thoughtful man can examine his own personality without being painfully conscious of inborn traits and hereditary tendencies which are a perpetual hindrance to his noble aspirations?

And if the average preponderance of physical im-
perfection, and intellectual mediocrity, and moral
obliquity be so deplorable, what are we to say to
the unpardonable amount of deformity, insanity,
idiocy, and viciousness that disfigures our streets
and fills our asylums, hospitals, and prisons? The
time is past for the plea of innate depravity as an
excuse for overt wickedness; the amiable superstition that idiots are under the special protection
of God must give way before a better knowledge
of the laws which govern pre-natal existence; the
wise ones of the race have already discovered that
children are made by their parents, not sent, with
all their imperfections on their head, from heaven.

The science of statistics, though yet in its dawn,
is beginning to throw light upon the causes of the
frequent failures and disasters that occur in the
propagation of the human species; by-and-by, let
us hope, the subject will receive at least as much
attention as is shown in the cultivation of vege-
tables and the improvement of breeds in dumb
animals. It was no freak of Nature nor favoritism
of Providence, but merely the unhindered opera-
tion of beneficent laws, that gave Shakspeare his
transcendent genius, that fashioned Milton as
beautiful in form as excellent in mental gifts and
graces, that singled out Benjamin Franklin from a
large family as "the one great, round, sound apple
on the tree."

All the gossips can chatter about the fright that

made a mother "mark" her unborn infant with a
beastly exterior or a vacant brain, and of some
ungratified "longing" of hers developed into a
corresponding bias towards evil in her child's
character, to the blighting of its after-career; but
how few, even among parents, learn wisdom from
a recognition of the exceptionally good health, or
strong love, or harmonious exaltation of feeling
on their own part, that set the seal of perfection
upon the fruit of some auspicious procreative act!

But, though this subject is, as yet, but little understood, certain principles have already been
adopted by general consent as so intimately connected with the welfare of the race, that they may
be considered as forming a ground for improvement
and a stand-point of responsibility in parentage.

One of the most obvious of these principles is,
the evil of marriage between near relatives, on
account of the degeneration likely to result there-
from. It would seem that there are people enough
in the world to choose from without marrying
among one's next of kin ; but family pride often
leads parents to urge a union between cousins in
order to consolidate property, and propinquity is
generally sufficient to awaken between the young
people themselves an affection which they mistake
for the attraction of a healthier choice. In Germany, an uncle sometimes marries his niece and
a nephew his aunt; such cases, however, occur
only among persons rich enough and influential

enough to obtain a special dispensation from the government. It is singular that the laws of England, which strictly prohibit marriage with a deceased wife's sister, should yet allow marriage between first cousins, which has been productive of so much degeneracy and disease in that country. There appears to be some neutralization of vital power in the offspring of persons near of kin, which leads to scrofula, consumption, and insanity; and when intermarrying is carried on for several generations, the race dies out for lack of heirs, or runs out gradually in the production of diminutive and inferior specimens of humanity.

There are plenty of instances of the truth of this assertion to be found in all wealthy and old-settled communities. In our own country they are to be found notably in the New England States, where the rigors of the climate and the highly electric state of the atmosphere serve to develop all tendencies to nervous disease, and where the strain upon the intelligence and capacity of all classes is a severe test of the vitality of each individual.

In the Old World, the lowest stratum of society is made up of beings so brutish and degraded, that the possession of a shade more or less of intelligence is scarcely to be noticed. The descendant of uncounted generations of ignorant forefathers is stupid and coarse, and no amount of training can make him wise and gentle. But in America, where there is no such thing as a peasant class, and where the worth of the individual, as such, is everywhere acknowledged, the lack of brains, or of blood, in a single specimen of the race is a positive loss to society; and hence it is in America that the keenest interest should be felt in the improvement of the species.

It is in the older portions of the United States that marriages between near relatives have been most common; indeed, there are districts where nearly all the inhabitants are related to each other in no very remote degree. A traveler in the eastern part of Maine came, a few years ago, upon a household bearing the name of one of the most extensive families in New England. The heads of this isolated branch—who were themselves own cousins, besides being related over and over again through the intermarriage of mutual ancestors— were extremely feeble-minded and feeble-bodied persons, having scarcely sense and strength enough to attend to the ordinary duties of a small farm; one of their children was capable of assisting them, two others were more like beasts than human beings, and were obliged to be penned up in separate corners of the room behind a kind of rude lattice, contrived by the parents for the protection of their wild and idiotic progeny. And in how many old New England families is there a remote chamber set apart for the crazy, or melancholy, or half-witted member, whom affection cannot bear to deliver over to the tender mercies of an asylum?

how many whose skeleton in the closet is the remembrance of a suicide, and the fear of an inherited
tendency to commit the same ghastly deed of
despair? how many in which the broken law
avenges itself in the milder curse of oddity, in an
apparent inability to follow the accustomed ways
of mankind? a peculiarity which is, as it were, a
caricature of the eccentricities of genius, and which
brings no renown to its possessor, since it is barren
of useful or beautiful results.

The State of New Hampshire, realizing the disastrous effects of the marriage of near relatives,
has lately passed a law prohibiting the union of
first cousins; an enactment the moral influence of
which will probably be more wide-spread than the
limits of its jurisdiction.

It would seem that an instinctive consciousness,
on the part of those near of kin who do marry,
that the act is wrong, or at least of doubtful pru-
dence, has something to do with the defects of
their offspring. There was probably a time in the
history of every tribe out of which a nation has
grown, when brothers and sisters intermarried for
lack of other partners. But either the race was
then vigorous enough to bear this fusion of kindred blood without injury, or the baleful effects of
the temporary transgression were gradually overcome by "the survival of the fittest" in the union
of such offspring with members of alien tribes.
However this may be, it is certain that the decline

of physical strength and the development of the
moral nature through civilization have rendered
the race of to-day unfit to bear any willful impov-
erishing of the vital forces.

Two curious instances, occurring within the past
generation in the United States, may be quoted in
support of the theory that in this matter the hesi-
tations of conscience increase the inevitable depression of natural power.

A certain couple who had met in adult life as
strangers discovered, after having been married
many years, during which period several children
had been born to them, that there was little doubt
of their being own brother and sister to each other.
Their parents having died when the children were
very young, and they having been adopted by
strangers and entirely separated while they were
growing up, made this complete loss of identifica-
tion possible. On becoming convinced of the truth
of their suspicions, their married life was at once
broken up; the wife remained with the children,
and the husband removed to a distance, although
friendly relations were kept up between all the
members of the family. Now, the children of this
innocently-incestuous marriage were not lacking
in physical or mental powers; so far as is yet
known, there was nothing remarkable about them
in any way; they were good average specimens of
the race.

But in the other case, of a family living alone in

a remote part of the country, the children cohabited freely, and *their* children were scarcely human in either form or intellect. The ability to propagate appeared to have ceased with the second generation.

There are, to be sure, instances where the children of cousins show no trace of weakness or lack of equilibrium in their temperaments ; just as there are instances of scrofula, consumption, insanity, and idiocy among the descendants of parents entirely unrelated to each other; but the fortunate exceptions in the former case are probably due to a dissimilarity in the constitutions of husband and wife, and the failures in the latter case to a lack of proper contrast, which may obtain even among strangers. The whole science of the question is yet in its infancy, but this much we already know, that in the marriage of cousins the chances are against the healthiness of offspring, while if the practice be continued through a second generation, the result is almost certain to be disastrous.

Again, it is the duty of all persons afflicted with scrofula, syphilis, consumption, or insanity not to marry, and to refrain altogether from propagating their kind. If marriage were prohibited to all in whom the slightest taint of these diseases is apparent or suspected, candidates for matrimony would be few indeed, since it is seldom that a perfectly healthy family, or even individual, can be found; but the children of delicate parents often outgrow their inherited feebleness, and through change of climate or judicious care are able to eliminate all vestiges of a curse from their offspring. Where, however, a family has become thoroughly saturated with the virus of any of the above-mentioned diseases,—so that its members show plainly in their outward appearance, in their ailments, and in their characters, that the inborn tendency is only waiting for time and circumstances to develop itself,—it is the duty of such a family not to hand down their misery any further. Who has not seen these unmistakable signs going straight through from one generation to another, in some cases appearing to grow weaker through the infusion of a new element into the tainted blood, in other cases predominating over every struggle for improvement, and breaking out at last into violent madness or incurable decay?

These pale babies with wan smiles and feeble motions; these frail children with sore eyes, discharging ears, and swollen throats; these youths and maidens with narrow chests and prematurely-awakened feelings, both sentimental and religious; these men and women with low heads, broad necks, square jaws, and loose lips, who carry danger in their flashing eyes, and destruction in the fitful leapings of their heated blood,—these are not the materials out of which to develop the, as yet, only partially-discovered possibilities of the human race.

Said one, in speaking of a young girl whose

acquaintance he had recently made: "Yes, she is certainly handsome; but there is in her face a peculiar look that repels me; she reminds me, somehow, of Jane Eyre's description of Rochester's mad wife!"

The girl, in truth, belonged to a race conspicuous for the cases of insanity, idiocy, and suicide that had occurred among its members for several generations; and although she herself had thus far shown no symptoms of disease, the taint was doubtless in her temperament, and displayed itself in her countenance.

A striking instance of the mischief produced by a lack of vitality in a parent took place a few years ago in a New England village. A woman of exceptionally vigorous health and corresponding nobleness of form, whose blooming face and cheerful equanimity of disposition seemed to radiate strength and peace upon all who approached her, married a man who was her equal in intelligence and goodness, but sadly her inferior in physical soundness, being the last survivor of a consumptive family, and afflicted himself with the same disease in the form which it often assumes in New England, namely, a slow decline, lasting for many years, and enabling its victim to creep about among his fellows almost to his last breath.

They had three children. The first child died from exhaustion soon after its birth; the second lingered nearly two years, always feeble and fre-

quently prostrated by terrible fits, to one of which
it at last succumbed; the third lived to be five
years old and died suddenly, to the relief, even
more than to the regret, of those interested in his
fate.

His organization was a remarkable exhibition of
the struggle between the two contrasted elements
—the one healthy, the other diseased—that had
given him being. From his mother he had inherited grandeur of form and beauty of feature, so
that at a short distance he was a magnificent
specimen of childhood. He looked like "a little
prince," as we republicans are fond of saying, from
our ideal notions of what a prince ought to be.
Nor would a nearer view have dispelled the charm,
had it not been for an unnatural wildness of eye
and restlessness of manner that changed the admiration of the beholder into surprise and almost
terror. A few moments' observation was sufficient
to carry the conviction that here was a completely
irrational and irresponsible being, not idiotic and
not crazed, but abnormal in all his intellectual and
moral functions. Although under the almost exclusive care of his mother, whose life was necessarily devoted to him, he was, from his determined
tendency to mischief, a source of constant anxiety
to the entire household. His whole nature seemed
to run to destructiveness. Knives, dishes, books,
whatever was within reach that he had strength
to lift, were thrown right and left without discrim-

ination or apparent object. Although the child of wealthy parents, his surroundings were obliged to be of the plainest : he ate from a metal plate ; the rooms he frequented were kept as bare as possible of movable furniture and ornaments; no toy appeared to give him pleasure, except while he was breaking it, and no domestic animal could be admitted to that hospitable hearth. And these destructive tendencies seemed only to grow with his growth and strengthen with his strength, while reason still slumbered, and affection could scarcely be said to exist in his nature. His father could do nothing with him; punishment was out of the question ; and what little influence his mother was able to exert, appeared to be more through the force of habit upon his mind than through any conscious yielding to her will.

And yet there were occasional gleams of intellect that showed how gifted a mind was wrecked within that beautiful body. His voice was remarkably sweet and powerful, and he had caught the tunes, though not the words (for at four years old he could not talk) of several hymns which his mother was in the habit of singing while putting him to sleep. Sometimes he would break out into one of these melodies, but it was rarely that he went through with it ; usually he would soon change his soft tones into the most piercing shrieks, apparently well pleased to witness the consternation aroused in his listeners by his per-

verse behavior. Even maternal tenderness could
not regard the early death of such a being as a
misfortune, since there was no prospect of any
improvement in his condition. In the absence of
any untoward incident during his mother's pregnancy, and with the additional proof afforded by
the unhealthiness and premature death of her other
offspring, it is only just to conclude that the blasting of these infant lives was due to the father's
diseased and exhausted state ; indeed, at the time
of the birth of the boy above described, he was far
advanced in consumption, and he died a few years
afterwards.

These persons, in marrying, did not know the
risks they were running nor the penalty they were
to pay ; but their sad experience ought to serve as
a warning to others, and help to put an end to the
injustice of calling into existence beings who, from
the very nature of the case, cannot be endowed
with a due portion of healthy vitality.

So also cretinism, which, whatever may be its
predisposing causes, always develops increased
horrors in the second generation, has been per-
petuated for ages in certain cantons of Switzerland
through the influence of the priests, who have
encouraged cretins to marry, and opposed as blasphemy and sacrilege all efforts on the part of
philanthropists and physicians to prevent the
spread of the evil through propagation. Indeed,
throughout Christendom the error has thus far

prevailed that the sanction of the Church is sufficient to hallow any union, no matter how completely its conditions may transgress the beneficent laws of Nature.

Again, the poor ought not to marry. No man and woman, however strong may be their love for one another, have any right to become parents until they have accumulated a sufficient provision for the comfortable maintenance and proper education of the children they may call into being. It is not only that what was decent poverty for the young couple while alone is likely to become want and starvation when the family is enlarged, but the offspring of such a union are deprived of their rights before their birth, through the meagre nourishment and excessive labors and sordid anxieties of their progenitors.

There is no virtue in bringing into the world a mass of puny, weak-minded, and vicious beings, such as the children of the very poor are likely, from their surroundings, to be or become; and yet, philosophers who show plainly that the sufferings of the poor are mainly the necessary result of their own imprudence, are cried out against as monsters of heartlessness and cruelty. The clergy encourage the multiplication of paupers by preaching sentimental sermons from the text, "The poor ye have always with you" (as though the words of Christ were a commandment instead of the simple statement of a fact), and calling frequently to mind the destitution of Jesus who had "not where to lay his head" (forgetting to note that he took care not to involve others in his homelessness); the statistical reporters of already over-burdened districts remark with pride the continual increase of the population; fictitious literature, by its attractive pictures of cleanly indigence, or its dramatic scenes of distress, dulls the comprehension of the better classes as to the real evils of poverty; and unwise charity offers, in effect, a premium to what ought to be considered unlawful and criminal parentage. So only that marriage lead the way to propagation, no further restraint is demanded. Thus, a few days ago, in Chicago, a man arrested on the charge of refusing to marry a servant-girl whom he had seduced, excused his desertion on the plea that he had not enough money to pay a magistrate the necessary trifling marriage-fee; whereupon the judge furnished the money, and the couple departed to be joined in "holy wedlock" and to increase the population of Chicago, not only by the infant so timely legitimatized, but, probably, by as many more children as usually fall to the lot of persons who marry young without any visible means of support.

In this instance no one appeared to consider the circumstances as deplorable. The complainant was satisfied with being made "an honest woman"; the defendant seemed willing to trust in the Providence that presides over new and sparsely populated countries; the judge, no doubt, thought he had done a generous deed, and the denizens of the court-room dismissed the matter as a good joke. It is in America, if anywhere, that such matters can be treated lightly; but the same indifference prevails to a great extent throughout the world. The poor of all nations say, " We cannot afford to divert ourselves as the rich do; we have only one resource of pleasure, the indulgence of sexual passion, and you would forbid us that!" And the rich say, "These poor people have the same instinct with ourselves to propagate their kind, and who would dare withstand Nature in this particular, when the indulgence is sanctioned by law and sanctified by religion?"

But Nature never agreed to feed children without food; and so, whenever and wherever the supply of nourishment is inadequate, Nature stunts and starves and brutalizes and slays without remorse the superfluous issue of her reproductive laws; nor can any amount of legislation or of charity avail so long as a disproportion between numbers and the ability to maintain them be suffered to exist. The French principle that no more children ought to be born to any couple than they are able to support is a right one, and must in the end obtain everywhere; but the French method of carrying the theory into practice is immoral, and the result, so far as the nation in the aggregate is concerned, is rendered partially null by the enormous number of illegitimate births occurring outside of these small families.

With regard to illegitimate children everywhere, it may be said that they are a loss to society. Not only are the physical and mental advantages with which, from being the offspring of violent passion, they might naturally be. gifted, neutralized in many cases by the fear and shame of the prospective mother, but they are apt to inherit the moral instability of their parents; while they are rarely offered an opportunity for the full development of their capacities, being either suffered to come up hap-hazard, through the charity of strangers, or subjected to the equalizing discipline of a foundling hospital, which does not profess to allow for the exceptional tastes or talents of individual members. The existence of such a class must always be a drawback to the moral elevation and a drain upon the physical resources of any nation; a stain and a hindrance which must, however, continue to afflict until a true sense of the sacredness of marriage and the responsibility of parentage shall be universally felt and acted upon.

Having thus rapidly denoted the particular cases in which moral obligation would forbid men and women to propagate their kind, we come lastly to that class of persons who, through the possession of a healthy organization and sufficient means of support, are at liberty to marry and become parents.

To such the principal warning must be: Do
NOT MARRY TOO YOUNG!—a piece of advice which,
if it had always been given and heeded, would
have prevented the evils which now forbid marriage in many instances, and make it a martyrdom
or a mockery to thousands who enter upon its
obligations. The statute legalizes marriages that
take place after both parties have reached the
average age of puberty, and people in general
seem to think that the earlier an attached pair are
settled in life the better. Mothers are ashamed
when their daughters remain on their hands' until
they are over twenty years old; and though sons
are expected to wait longer, since they are the
bread-winners of the new household, it is tacitly
understood that they are likely to gratify their
propensities in the mean time by illicit connections.
In the United States there is great temptation to
marry early, on account of the ease of procuring a
livelihood, but the practice is in many ways disastrous in its effects.

In the first place, the physical powers require
several years' development, after the crisis of
puberty is passed, before either sex is able to
contribute its best strength in the creation of
offspring. It is a great mistake to suppose that
the awakening of sexual inclination implies the
presence of sexual power. Nature's law of increase
is so necessary to her whole economy, that she
whispers to each individual of future obligations

long before she would have such obligations
assumed; and Nature herself is forestalled in this
regard by the corruptions of society. It is marvelous to see how early children who are not
properly taken care of betray a consciousness of
the mystery of sex, and how the passions can
become prematurely awakened through vicious
companionship and prurient literature. It would
seem in many instances that the child has been
born with a decided bias towards lust. This is
doubtless the fact, and the blame is to be laid
directly upon the parents who, through ignorance
or selfishness, hesitated not to inflame the dormant
spirit of their unborn infant with the fires of their
own frequent passion. And this wrong is more
apt to be committed by *young* married persons
than by those who with years have acquired self-
mastery.

If, as we all know to be true, the physical and
mental traits of parents can be separately, or com-
binedly, inherited by their offspring; nay, if even
a mother's accidental longing for, or dislike of,
some particular article of food during her pregnancy can impress her child for its lifetime with a
corresponding taste as regards the same dish, who
can doubt that the sexual appetite, which concerns
so intimately both mind and body, may become
an abnormally powerful element in a character
compounded of persons whose blood is habitually
agitated by the stimulus of desire?

Of course there are many other conditions besides abstinence from sexual gratification which are
necessary to the production of desirable offspring,
but there is not one of these, whether relating to
physical health or mental culture in the parents,
but is more likely to be observed by persons of
mature years than by the very young.

It is impossible to determine in what proportion
a father is responsible for the natural tendencies of
his child; but it is certain that for the development
of these natural tendencies, both before birth and
during the first years of independent existence, the
mother's influence is almost unlimited, and it is,
therefore, to the mother that one is inclined to
apply all rules for the improvement of the race.
Good mothers are generally found behind the
glory of good and great men; and if the secret
history of each of these women could be known,
we should probably discover that her solicitude
for her child's welfare began while she held his
being under the control of her own pulses.

The physical beauty and mental harmony of the
ancient Greeks was largely due to the universal
care taken to influence their pregnant women
through beautiful objects and harmonious sounds,
and this pre-natal advantage was supplemented by
a judicious training of the whole being, in order
that each individual might approximate as nearly
as possible to the high ideal of that wonderful
race.

"It is related that before the birth of Confucius, his mother, aware that she was to be the parent of a sage, took every means to give perfection to the character of her unborn child. After his birth she went to dwell in the neighborhood of sepulchres, that he might be taught sympathy and pity. She afterwards located herself near a butcher's shop, that he might be taught the useful arts of life. She then changed her domicile so as to be next door to a school, that he might witness the rewards of diligence."

How true to the echo of these wise instructions are the precepts of the illustrious teacher whose disciples outnumber, even to this day, the followers of any other religious leader!

"*To know what is just and not to practice it, is cowardice.*"

"*Judge yourself severely, and judge others indulgently ; so shall you be secured against ill will.*"

"*He is a true man who, in the sight of profit, thinks of justice,—of danger, risks his life ; and who, without obligation, remembers a promise he has made.*"

"*What you would not that others should do to you, do not you to them.*"

So, also, in the case of Hiouen-thsang, the Chinese scholar, who, more than twelve hundred years ago, performed the perilous and, at that time, almost unheard-of journey to India, in order to study the system of Buddha. It was

his mother's influence upon his character before,
as well as after, his birth, that led him to the
undertaking and sustained his courage under its
difficulties and dangers, from which his companions soon turned back in despair.

" His mother had told him"—so runs the record
—"that shortly before giving birth to him she had
seen her child traveling to the Far West in search
of the Law." And his own youth was haunted by
the same visions, the reflection of her fond and
pious picturings of his future career.

The soul of Mary, the mother of Jesus, magni-
fied the Lord, and her spirit rejoiced in God her
Saviour, in view of her approaching maternity.
What wonder that her first-born was called "the
Son of the Highest," and caused her to become
forever "blessed among women"?

Well would it be if every prospective mother
everywhere and throughout all time could have
faith to believe that she is "to be the parent of a
sage," and reverence to feel that the being she
carries beneath her heart is a "holy thing!"

Unfortunately, there are not lacking instances
equally striking of children born to do evil,
through the reflected power of their mother's
wicked thoughts and deeds.

During the War of Emancipation, a Southern
lady who, with her child and her property, had fled
to the North for safety, was obliged to consult a
certain eminent physician concerning the tenden-

cies of this only child, a boy of three years, who was already so malignant in his disposition and so murderously inclined towards all who approached him, whenever he could get at a knife or scissors or any sharp instrument, that he was the terror of every public and private house in which she sought to take up her abode. The physician, after watching the boy for a short time, exclaimed, "Madam, this child was ruined before his birth: I cannot help him now!" The lady then confessed that during her pregnancy she had been in a state of continual excitement with regard to the war, and had yielded without restraint to the bitterness of her feelings against the North. She had spent most of the time in a Southern city which was occupied by Union troops, and whenever she saw an officer or a soldier wearing the detested uniform, she had longed to kill him, and had enjoyed in imagination the act of plunging a dagger into his heart.

And this was the result of her foolish spite! Her child, if he live, will probably always need to be kept under restraint, and his perverted nature will therefore die with him; but in many other cases the mischief is handed down to children's children, and curses thousands outside the circle of kinship.

A curious and suggestive fact has recently been recorded in New York, which may be quoted here in illustration of this subject.

About seventy years ago, in a small village in northern New York, a young girl was left adrift, who subsequently led a wandering life, subsisting almost entirely upon the charity of the inhabitants. "She became the mother of a long race of criminals and paupers, and her progeny has cursed the county ever since. The county records show two hundred of her descendants who have been criminals. In one single generation of her unhappy line there were twenty children; of these, three died in infancy, and seventeen survived to maturity. Of the seventeen, nine served in the state prisons for high crimes an aggregate term of fifty years, while the others were frequent inmates of jails, penitentiaries, and almshouses." Now, although the poverty and ignorance in which the descendants of this girl were allowed to grow up had much to do with their disgraceful history, there can be no doubt that a peculiar tendency to lawlessness and crime was the special legacy of their common maternal ancestor,—the direct result of her exceptionally hardened nature and abandoned career.

The mother of Goethe was under twenty years of age when her son was born, but his father was much older; and, while the exuberant health and joyous spirits of the mother probably contributed largely to the remarkable beauty and vitality of their offspring, the thoughtful reticence and stern dignity of the father's character may have had

most to do with his transcendent intellectual
powers.   Goethe himself says:

"Vom Vater hab' ich die Statur
Des Lebens ernstes Führen;
Vom Mütterchen die Frohnatur
Und Lust zum Fabuliren."

It is a fact, proved by statistics founded upon the
observations of many years in various parts of the
world, that children born of mothers between the
ages of twenty-four and twenty-nine are *longer*
than those born of younger mothers; and this
superiority in stature at birth implies a corre-
spondingly greater development in the whole
being of the infant.   It has long been a noticeable
fact that, while women who marry very young
breed rapidly, as a rule, their children are neither
strong nor long-lived.   We hear a great deal now-
adays about the large families of former times,
when women were not afraid of the troubles of
maternity, and men were proud of a long line of
sons and daughters.   But whoever traces the
history of such families will see that, on an average, not half of the children born lived to grow
up, and still fewer of those who survived were of
any special benefit to the world except in the way
of increasing its numbers.   The records of the nobility in all aristocratic countries show a striking
percentage of infant deaths, although in families
of rank the children would be nourished with

peculiar care. And an attentive observer of old monuments and genealogical paintings will notice that a large proportion of the numerous groups of little ones that surround heads of households carry in their hands *the skull surmounted by a red cross*, denoting that they died before their parents. In a village churchyard in Yorkshire, England, is a stone to the memory of eleven children of Richard ——, who all " died young;" and so on, to six children of another, and nine children of another. And in Forster's " Life of Dickens" it is related that the tombstones whose inscriptions to five little children so worked upon the feelings of poor Pip, in " Great Expectations," are actually standing in a churchyard near Rochester, and record the death of *twelve* children instead of five.

Now and then, in our own day, is to be found a mother who is the pride of her home and of all the region round about, because she has given birth to an extraordinary number of children. The writer recalls an instance of a woman who had had twenty-three children at the full term, and, counting miscarriages, had been a mother *thirty-two* times. And how many children had she succeeded in raising? *Six;* and two of these were delicate !

But some persons, perhaps the greater majority, will say, " What matter if so many of these died prematurely? Their mother may rejoice in the thought that she has presented more than a score of infant angels to the family of heaven !"

Here again comes in the pernicious " other-world-liness" that has hindered the progress of the human race in so many ways. The truth is, we know nothing whatever about heaven; but we do know, or ought to know, that what is wanted for *this* world is children born with vitality enough not to tax the utmost endeavors of a whole family to keep them alive, and who will stay on the earth long enough to do the work of their own generation, and pass it on to capable successors.

It is impossible that any two parents should be able to bestow upon a dozen children the physical strength and intellectual capacity that they could give to half or a quarter as many. It is seldom that both parties of a twin birth survive, and still more seldom that both or either of them possess more than average abilities; triplets and other multitudinous births are now rightly looked upon as monstrosities. And, on the same principle, the birth of a child every year, or within any period inadequate to the complete recovery of vigor on the part of the mother, is an outrage upon all immediately concerned and a wrong to posterity.

The principal newspapers of London publish a list of births, usually from ten to fifteen daily, occurring in families of the upper and middle classes. Although the circumstances in such cases are as favorable as can exist, there is scarcely a day when one or two or three "still-births" are not recorded; while the great proportion of still-births among the lower classes is frequently made the topic of anxious discussion in the medical journals.

If women would wait until they are twenty-five years old before marrying, their children would be fewer in number and more vigorous in body and mind than the great majority of human beings are at present. Even in cases of extreme fecundity, the tendency lessens with years; so that she who between the ages of sixteen and thirty-two might give birth to sixteen children, would not be likely between the ages of twenty-five and forty-five to give birth to more than eight, and these eight would be likely to be worth twice as much as the earlier sixteen.

And not only are the children of early marriages likely to be born inferior, but the degree of care and kind of training that they are pretty sure to receive lessen the chances that remain of their growing up helps and blessings to their contemporaries. Most girls, especially in America, marry before they have themselves outlived the period of thoughtless gayety. Not only are they physically too immature to produce vigorous offspring, but they are not fitted by disposition or experience to undertake the training of a child. Hence the majority of little ones are ruined by over-indulgence during infancy; and as soon as they are a little older are packed off to school to keep them out of the way, so that those early years, which determine the character for the whole life, are comparatively uninfluenced by the person who has the best right and the best opportunity to set the seal of her own convictions upon the choices of her child. Where there is a large family and not much money to support it, the mother is forced to neglect the individual wants of her children in order to provide for their aggregate needs; where there are many children and great wealth, there is apt to be a strong staff of hirelings to attend to the juvenile members of the household, that the young mother may be free to follow her, as yet, unextinguished love of worldly pleasure. Now, while there is scarcely a young girl of sixteen or eighteen years old to be found who, in looking forward to marriage, considers maternity as the crowning glory of that state, there is scarcely an unmarried woman of twenty-five who is not conscious of the maternal instinct, and ready to welcome, with the wedded affection of her lover, the privilege of giving birth to, and caring for, his children. Setting all other conditions aside, who can doubt that, with this difference of opinion to start with, the latter class of wives would make the better mothers?

But many will say, "No matter how giddy a girl may be, as soon as she actually becomes a mother the true mother-love will be awakened." There are incidents occurring every day which prove that this assumption is not true. The maternal instinct is like every other human affection; it has its own time for a right development, and, if created prematurely, it will fail either partially or wholly. Perpetual maidenhood does not necessarily quench this pure fire; it more frequently turns it from the narrow hearth of home, and diffuses its warmth and light over the outside world. All great enterprises for the relief of the sick, the needy, the homeless; all endeavors for the abolishment of war; all political reforms for the amelioration of civil and social wrongs, are largely due to the exertions of single women; while there is scarcely a household wherein the young folks do not appeal from the occasional injustice of parents to the unworn sympathies of a maiden aunt.

It is sad to see a withered virgin caressing with unspoken yearnings the placid infant or merry child of her happy matron friend; it is sadder to see a young wife harassed and exhausted with her prematurely assumed maternal duties, until she denounces children as plagues and torments, and congratulates her childless neighbors on their freedom from such cares.

"You have a large family?" said a benevolent visitor to the wife of an English laborer.

"Yes, madam; but, God be thanked, we have buried a many childer, for all that we ha' gotten such a ruck on 'em left. I often tells my husband belike God will be so koind to tak most of these too, and rid our hands o' the care on 'em!"

Again, in too youthful marriages the partners are not often mated in tastes and dispositions, and

the "unsuitability of mind and purpose" becomes
more and more apparent as the characters of both
are developed.   From the stand-point of this article, unhappy marriages are to be deplored chiefly
on account of the injury done to children through
a lack of harmonious affection in the parents.

Temperance in sexual indulgence may prevent
the marriage-bed from becoming "dull, stale, tired,"
and its issue from being a "tribe of fops;" but the
husband and wife who outrage love by yielding to
passion when their hearts are full of mutual hatred
or repulsion cannot hinder the wrong from taking
effect in the chilled affections and morbid tempers
of their offspring.   Life is sure to be hard enough
and sorrowful enough to the being born with every
advantage of natural temperament.   It is the es-
sence of cruelty to summon into existence creatures
whose dispositions are soured and embittered in
the very outset through the reflected enmity of
their progenitors.

It is a fact that among the most enlightened
peoples of the world at the present day there is a
wide-spread and continually increasing disinclina-
tion to raise large families.   Rich men, in these
times of precarious enterprises and huge speculations, prefer to have only a small group of
direct heirs to inherit their wealth or share their
possible bankruptcy; rich women prefer to spare
a portion of their time and strength for the
enjoyment of a life so full of resources as theirs

may be, instead of devoting their best years entirely to the pains and cares of maternity; persons in moderate circumstances feel the necessity of a liberal education for their children, and, therefore, deprecate the appearance of a greater number than their purses are able to support; the poor, for whom the world has every day less and less room, feel more and more each addition to their respective families to be a burden rather than a blessing.

In England there are not wanting brave voices to declare, " This reckless and unbounded propagation ought to cease !" Even in Germany, where the *frau* is supposed to be constantly and contentedly occupied in making soup, knitting stockings, and rocking the cradle, the women of the upper classes are beginning to rebel against the too frequent drain upon their powers in the office of maternity; and in America, while mothers joyfully bestow their daughters in marriage before they are fit to be out of the school-room, it is usually with the hope, expressed or felt, that the young wife may "enjoy her liberty" for a few years before settling down to the cares of a nursery. And with this often selfish desire to escape trouble, there is manifest a growing reference to the welfare of offspring.

The following extract from a highly respectable and widely read weekly journal in the United States is very suggestive :

"And if they don't want to be troubled with children, let 'em grow till they are three months old, and then drown 'em ; but don't get rid of them in a cowardly fashion beforehand. That's what reduces a woman's health and submits her to slow decay. I wish you'd tell 'em that! A woman has no business to have a string of children long enough to go across the street; but she ought to have one or two. And she is, above all things, to be pitied who destroys her first-born. If she ever has a fine, intelligent child, it should be the first, and in losing that she cuts down the flower and hope of her life."

Now, these remarks were written in good faith, and for the purpose of dissuading the numerous fashionable ladies with whom the paper is a favorite from injuring their health and wounding their consciences by committing the crime of fœticide. Yet even this humane "doctor," who has sufficient faith in the strength of maternal instinct to feel quite safe in proposing that unwilling mothers should drown their babies after allowing them to live three months, recognizes the principle that a woman ought not to have "a string of children long enough to go across the street."

So, too, a certain New England divine, whose orthodoxy is above suspicion, said, a few years ago, in a public address, "So far as I can see, it would be much more for the glory of God to make fewer human beings and make them better." And then added piously, " but I feel faith in God, who knows best !"

It is well that the Christian system displays God as more attentive to motive than to action,—to feeling rather than to its expression in words; otherwise how could a more horrible blasphemy be uttered than is contained in the above quotation ? " *Make*," indeed !

Even the Mormons, whose system appears at first sight to be wholly an apotheosis of lust, ought to have credit for two of their fundamental principles: one, the right of every woman to become a mother; the other, the right and duty of every pregnant woman to remain undisturbed by sexual intercourse during the whole period of gestation.

Any person interested in the subject cannot fail to observe that the current literature of our day is assuming a less superstitious and more scientific tone in treating of parental responsibility, as well as every other topic connected with the welfare of society.

It cannot be denied that the gradual change of sentiment and elevation of motive with regard to human propagation is the result of increased knowledge, of enlarged education, in both sexes and among all classes.

The most earnest champions of the rights of unborn children are to be found (as is the case in all reforms) among the minority of thinkers who dare

to stand outside of the established pale of religious
and social rules and customs.   It is the men and
women who have ceased to consider themselves
competent to declare what " God" is thinking and
willing and doing, and who do not venture to lay
the consequences of human ignorance and reck-
lessness upon *the mysterious workings of an inscru-
table Providence*, who have been the first to assert
that parents are themselves responsible for the
status of their children at birth as well as for the
subsequent development of their characters.

There are no more judicious and conscientious
mothers on earth than are to be found among the
leaders of the "Woman's Rights movement"; it is
not in that class of women that one may seek
successfully for degenerate homes and neglected
nurseries.   Nay, even the " Free-Lovers," whose
defiance of social laws has banished them from
professedly moral communities, have sent out from
their lonely island in Lake Champlain their ulti-
matum in the maxim, " PARENTAGE IS DIVINE."
There is hope that a society which starts with
such a principle will, with better knowledge, attain
to a higher standard than the theory of promiscuous alliances; there is no hope for a community
wherein public opinion sanctions the evasion of
the natural consequences of sexual union, and
considers parentage as anything less than "divine."

The greatest hindrance to any improvement in
the relations of the sexes lies in the supposed

strength of the sexual passion in man, rendering
it impossible for him to deny himself the pleasure
of that appetite, or even to delay its gratification
till marriage, without resorting to the compromise
of illicit connections.

That the sexual passion in man is, as a rule,
exceedingly strong, cannot be denied. The legends
of rude people turn largely upon struggles for the
possession of women, that the baser quality of love
may be satisfied, and all written history is full of
crimes springing from lust. Wise men in every age
have deplored the dominion of the flesh, and the
various attempts to kill out this rapacious instinct
have only resulted in the creation of new monstrosities in vice. One of the most spiritually-
minded of English divines confesses that Chris-
tians have no greater account than what must be
reckoned for "at the audit of concupiscence;" and
a recent valuable work on morals devotes its most
earnest and eloquent passage to a mournful recognition of the necessity for the existence of public
women, in order that the virtue of the home and
the family may be kept intact.

But the fact that men have always been licentious is no proof that they will always be so. It is
often quoted as a marked feature of the superiority
of the human race over the brute creation that,
while the lower animals are moved by the instinct
of propagation only during special seasons, man is
free to seek his mate whenever he chooses. But

monkeys are remarkable for this same freedom
and for its abuse; and in these days it does not
require a great stretch of imagination to consider
the tendency to excessive sensuality in man as due
to the continued culture of what an English writer
calls "the apish side of our nature."

Among primitive tribes, as among savages at
present, sexual passion was held in check to some
degree by the hardships of existence, by the fatigues
of the chase, and the ambition of excelling in games
of strength and bold exploits of war, rather than
by mental and moral discipline of the instinct;
while, on the other hand, with the progress of
civilization the admonitions of increasing knowledge have been deprived of much of their weight
by the enervation of the will through the refinements of social life. In both conditions, however,
woman has always stood ready to be the slave of
man's desires; and this fact is enough to explain
all the excesses of the past and present, while the
prospect of the complete emancipation of woman
is a sufficient ground for hope of the gradual purification of both sexes in the future.

For woman has never been a merely passive
agent in the sexual history of the race. It is
generally assumed that passion is much weaker
in the female than in the male of the human
species, but a careful observation of facts would
seem to show that the difference is entirely in
training. Many courtesans follow their infamous

trade because they enjoy it; and many girls called "virtuous" are so not from choice, but because restraining circumstances are too powerful for them to overcome. Many nuns have gone mad or sunk into premature decline on account of the strength of ungratified passion, and many more have saved themselves from such a fate by the voluntary sacrifice of the ostensible motive of their retirement from the world.

Continence is not a matter of sex, but of temperament and will and habit; and the fact that the vast majority of women are chaste in outward conduct is due to the force of public opinion, which does not allow them to be otherwise without condemnation, just as the fact that the vast majority of men are unchaste is due to there having been heretofore no tribunal to call them to account for their sins against purity. And yet, notwithstanding the absence of social penalties for this vice in their case, and the constant temptations to its committal, more men preserve their virginity until marriage, and even through life, than could be expected. The confidential advice of a mother who does not allow false modesty to keep her silent towards the son of her womb, with respect to the inward desires and outward allurements that will surely assail him at maturity, has saved many a young man from profaning his idea of the sex to which that mother belongs, and fraternal affection has enabled many a brother to see a sister in every woman until he has selected one of their number as his wife. There are also men in all classes who, without any especial home guidance, but with a definite and worthy object early in view, keep their minds pure from lust and their bodies in due subjection. There are priests who do not abuse the confidence of their flocks; monks who are really devoted to spiritual contemplation; scholars who cannot be charmed away from their intellectual researches by any devices of the tempter; philanthropists who dedicate to the good of the whole race the affections which they will not allow to centre upon an individual object; artisans and laborers to whom native modesty supplies the place of philosophy and conscious self-sacrifice in the struggle against the allurements of the flesh.

To every uncorrupted mind the highest ideal for man and woman is sexual purity. It is the virgin knight who finds the "Holy Grail," and Lohengrin is invincible because he is immaculate. Even the "Mother of God" must be further ennobled by the title of "Ever-Virgin," and Jesus owes the greater share of his influence as a reformer of morals to the fact that his name has never been associated with that of any woman.

The feeling which underlies so many beautiful legends of this kind is an instinctive one, and is a refreshing testimony to the supremacy of our spiritual over our physical nature. Love is sym-

pathy and mutual aspiration; passion is the con-
centration of physical power for the preservation of
the species. The first movement of love in either
sex is a seeking for congenial companionship, for
a depth of affection which friendship cannot im-
part. Later comes the desire of a more material
union; and, latest of all, the wish to call into existence a being who shall blend the distinctive traits
of its parents into a new form and character.

The more thoroughly man understands the
wants of his nature, the more clearly does he
perceive that the sexual passion is best served
when it is seldom exercised, and that it becomes
a debasing influence so soon as it is diverted from
its primal intention. For though the natural impulse towards the act has not in view its possible
ultimate result, still less does it contemplate the
avoidance of that result; and hence the performance of that act, accompanied by a deliberate
intention of escaping from its consequences, is
unnatural and immoral.

No married pair who resort to any of the
methods of "prevention" can reverence each other
as they might if their most sacred intercourse
were conducted innocently; and in the mind of
the man who frequents the society of courtesans,
the knowledge of their abnormal sterility is a
stronger element in the corruption of his moral
sense than is the memory of their vile conversation and promiscuous lewdness.

Within the last twenty years the emancipation of women has advanced more rapidly than during ages of earlier times. It is only natural that this sudden increase of liberty for the whole sex should be taken by individuals as an encouragement to license, particularly with reference to the conduct of life in love, marriage, and parentage. Women who have married unwisely in their early girlhood now seek to throw off the yoke and save a portion of their lives from the wreck of their fancied happiness; women who feel themselves competent to be the companions of their husbands in intellectual pursuits or political cares, marry with a determination to avoid the hindrances of maternity; wives who have already borne children are tired of the grave responsibilities and petty annoyances which these occasion, and are resolved to prevent any further increase of their families.

But the very facts of these cases prove that it is not knowledge, but the lack of it, which causes the mischief. The women who find in divorce the tardy remedy for their domestic misery are not to blame for seeking to free themselves from a life of "legal prostitution," but for ever having entered upon such a life; and their fault was occasioned by the want of sufficient occupation and of a judicious education during the years when the senses are most keen and the sentiments have not yet learned to obey the guidance of reason. Women who have no desire to undertake the office of maternity should know better than to marry until time shall have developed this peculiarly feminine side of their nature, and they recognize the instinctive desire to possess an object which shall be theirs exclusively, to nourish and train up for a future generation. Women who do not wish to have a large family should know, to begin with, that there is no justifiable mode of prevention excepting abstinence from sexual gratification. Any device which permits the indulgence of passion with immunity from its natural result is in most cases injurious to physical health, and in all a shock to moral purity, since conscience is thereby compromised.

In Victor Hugo's account of the nuptials of Cosette and Marius, the chastely-sensuous description of the wedding-night culminates in the suggestive sentence, "A little after midnight the Gillenormand mansion became a temple."

And so, in every marriage-chamber, whenever are performed

"The rites mysterious of connubial love,"

the oblation must be a free gift, the offering of sincere hearts, otherwise love is outraged at the very altar. The chaste bed of two wedded lovers, whether it be fruitful or not, is an object to awaken the purest sentiments of poetry and romance in a virgin breast; but who can deny that the whole idea of a union so close is profaned when the

sleeping-chamber is known to contain among the
paraphernalia of the toilet any of the modern in-
ventions for cheating Nature of her most glorious
triumph?

Hannah More relates that when, a fortnight after
the death of Garrick, she returned with his widow
to the house where the pair had lived so peacefully
together, she was surprised to see Mrs. Garrick go
alone into the chamber and bed in which he had
died. "I asked her the next day how she went
through it? She told me very well; that she first
prayed with great composure, then went and kissed
the dear bed, and got into it with a sad pleasure."

We may be sure that the sorrowful woman took
with her to that desolate couch a conscience void
of offense as to the most intimate relations of her
childless yet happy union.

The custom which now obtains in America, and
is sure to become prevalent everywhere, of edu-
cating the sexes together, not only in the nursery
and in primary schools but throughout all depart-
ments of university instruction, is the strongest
safeguard for the purity of future homes, and the
best surety for the progressive development of the
race. This good era has already dawned upon us;
but, so far as the women of the present generation
are concerned, it is not too much to say that the
majority of them are still in the bonds of ignorance, victims, more or less conscious, of early
mismanagement. Girlhood, which is always re-

ferred to by matrons as the most joyous period of
a woman's life, is not so in fact, because it is
tormented by the vague unrest of awakened and
undisciplined feeling, and made anxious by the
foolish haste to acquire an "establishment." Love
without care, marriage without children,—such is
the young girl's programme of future happiness,
and the attempt to realize these dreams produces
immeasurable disaster. "*Love is but an accident
in your lives; it is our whole existence,*" says the
fictitious heroine to the fictitious hero, as though
the admission were not in itself a condemnation of
her false position. No kind of happiness was ever
yet attained through making it the end and object
of pursuit; if it come, it comes as the reward of
duty conscientiously fulfilled, the accompaniment
of labor honestly performed.

And this is where most women make the grand
mistake of their lives. They do not spend their
youth in the cheerful accomplishment of the work
that lies nearest to them, and in the unembarrassed
enjoyment of the pleasures that belong to their
years, but they waste their time and dissipate their
fancy by indulging dreams of an impossibly beautiful future with an equally unreal partner. The
idle, peevish daughter expects to preside with
dignity and grace over a household of her own;
the selfish, impatient sister has no doubt of being
able to live in perpetual harmony with somebody
else's brother; the girl who will not strive for

excellence even in the accomplishments which she
looks upon as weapons of victory in her husband-
hunting campaign, expects to be worshiped all
her life by the gifted and cultured man whom she
pictures as her home-companion.

But the girls of succeeding generations will be
wiser; and one secret of their wisdom will consist
in the fact that their education will be secular,—
"godless," as the ultra-religionists call it.

There has been heretofore altogether too much
"other-worldliness" in the schedule of instruction,
and this has been particularly the case with regard
to women. The wonderful economy of nature has
been neglected in order to give prominence to the
system of Grace. The argument that sin must be
refrained from because its commission is an offense
against an invisible and extra-mundane God rarely
holds as a sufficient restraint in times of fierce
temptation, and is still further weakened by the
assurance of pardon in event of transgression.

Said a young married woman to an intimate
friend, when speaking of her suspicion that she
was pregnant, "I would rather not have a child at
present, but I should not dare make away with it,
for fear that afterwards I should be sorry."

Now, this woman, although uncommonly rever-
ential and devoted in religious matters, left her
acquired piety entirely out of sight in considering
her position, and spoke only from the instincts of
her nature. She did not say, "I am afraid the

deed would be wicked and would displease God," but "*I am afraid I should afterwards be sorry!*" She was rather below than above the average of her sex in intellectual ability, but was, without knowing it, one of those born mothers whose whole being is willingly absorbed in the work of maternity; and, though she was sufficiently affected by the careless and ignorant notions prevalent in these days concerning the responsibilities of woman in parentage to argue the question of acceptance or rejection of her future duties, she still felt that, should she evade her offered privilege, she would afterwards regret her loss.

But women of stronger intellect are in more danger of going astray, because they have room in their minds for many other interests, and the maternal instinct is apt to be long in developing; and with a keen intellect goes generally a strong will that is disposed to bend all things to its plans.

You cannot scare such women by threatening them with the Divine displeasure; they cannot be made to believe that the destruction of an embryo is a loss to an omnipotent Creator; and, as for themselves, the logical conclusion from the scheme of redemption is, "The greater the sinner the more glorious the salvation!"

But when women learn, through an early knowledge of their physical conformation, through a healthy development of their emotions, through an intelligent observation of the analogies of

nature in every department of animal and vege-
table life, the beautiful adaptation of their whole
being to the office of maternity, they will see that
to frustrate the process which leads to the crowning dignity of their sex would be not only to
inflict a wrong upon an unconscious victim, but
to strike a deadly blow at their own peace and
happiness.

The woman of the future will marry late and
bring few children into the world, but she will
form her offspring in serenity and thankfulness,
and no willful blasting of a germ shall be possible
even to her thought.

As woman becomes free and wise and self-sus-
taining, she will demand the same purity of man
that has always been demanded of herself; and
if, in her subjection, her influence has been so
immense both for evil and for good, how much
greater will be her power when she is universally
regarded as man's equal, and has strength to prefer
for herself and for him the path of innocence and
honor!

It is not difficult to imagine a future state of
society, when life shall have become so rich in resources for the ennobling of human nature, so full
of pure enjoyment, that the pleasure attendant upon
the animal function of reproduction shall never be
sought as an end, and the sexual act shall be
indulged in only at rare intervals, for the purpose
of calling into existence a sufficient number of

successors to the joyous inheritance of health, beauty, wisdom, and plenty, which shall have made the earth a Paradise,—a Paradise won by slow degrees through the errors and failures of countless generations; our own, alas! not being the last nor least in sinning and suffering in order to the final perfection of the race.

A MAGNIFICENT WORK.

A CRITICAL DICTIONARY OF ENGLISH LITERATURE

· AND

BRITISH AND AMERICAN AUTHORS,

LIVING AND DECEASED.

From the Earliest Accounts to the Latter Half of the Nineteenth Century. Containing over Forty-six Thousand Articles (Authors), with Forty Indexes of Subjects.

BY S. AUSTIN ALLIBONE.

Complete in Three Volumes, Imperial 8vo. 3140 pages. Price per vol.: Extra Cloth, $7.50; Library Sheep, $8.50; Half Turkey, $9.50.

OPINIONS ON THE MERITS OF THE WORK.

" As the work of a single man it is one of the wonders of literary industry. EVERY MAN WHO EVER OWNED AN ENGLISH BOOK, OR EVER MEANS TO OWN ONE, WILL FIND SOMETHING HERE TO HIS PURPOSE."—*Atlantic Monthly.*

" Far superior to any other work of the kind in our language."—*Lord Macaulay.*

" All things considered, the most remarkable literary work ever executed by one man."—*American Literary Gazette.*

" It may be safely said that it is the most valuable and comprehensive manual of English literature yet compiled."—*New York Evening Post.*

" There seems to be no doubt that the book will be welcomed to innumerable reading beings."—*Thomas Carlyle.*

" As a bibliographical work it is simply priceless."—*New York Independent.*

" We are proud that it is the work of an American. We earnestly recommend every reader, student and teacher, and, we had almost said, every patriotic citizen, to secure a copy of Allibone's Dictionary of Authors."—*Boston Evening Transcript.*

" A monument of unsparing industry, indefatigable research, sound and impartial judgment and critical acumen."—*Washington Irving.*

" These volumes are treasuries of English literature, without which no collection of books in our mother-tongue can be considered in any way satisfactory. They contain what can be possessed in no other way than by the ownership of whole libraries of books."—*Philadelphia Ledger.*

" If the rest of the work is as ably executed as that embraced under the first three letters of the alphabet, it cannot fail to be an important contribution to English literature."—*W. H. Prescott.*

" No dictionary of the authors of any language has ever before been undertaken on so grand a scale. For convenience and trustworthiness this work is probably not surpassed by any similar production in the whole range of modern literature. The author has erected a monument of literary industry of which the country has reason to be proud."—*New York Tribune.*

" In the English names alone Mr. Allibone's Dictionary will be far more complete than any work of the kind published in the country."—*London Daily News.*

Dr. William Smith, who is accorded to be one of the greatest compilers of the present age, has paid to the work of Mr. Allibone this generous tribute : " I have frequently consulted it, and have always found what I wanted. The information is given in that clear style and condensed form which is so important in a dictionary."

" Very important and very valuable."—*Charles Dickens.*

Special Circulars, containing a full description of the work, with specimen pages, will be sent, post-paid, on application.

Advice to a Wife on the Management of her own

Health, and on the Treatment of some of the Complaints incidenta! to Pregnancy, Labor and Suckling; with an Introductory Chapter especially addressed to a Young Wife. By PYE HENRY CHAVASSE, M.D. Eighth edition, revised. 16mo. Neatly bound in cloth. $2.00.

'From this advice any woman may gather some precious ideas as to the care of her health. The manual is very popular in England, where it has passed through eight rapid editions, and we know of no similar work where an equal amount of

doctor's lore is given in the style of plain modern conversation."—*Philada. Even Bulletin.*

"Possesses undoubted value for those to whom it is addressed."—*Chicago Journal.*

Advice to a Mother on the Management of her

Children, and on the Treatment on the moment of some of their more pressing Illnesses and Accidents. By PYE HENRY CHAVASSE, M.D. Ninth edition, revised. 16mo. Neatly bound in cloth. $1.50.

"For such, and for those who want to rear children judiciously, but need proper counsel, the present volume is one of the most valuable treatises ever published. The new edition contains many new notes,

and has undergone a careful revision by Sir Charles Locock, the first physician-accoucheur to Queen Victoria." — *N.Y Even. Post.*

Counsel to a Mother: Being a Continuation and

the Completion of "Advice to a Mother." By PYE HENRY CHAVASSE, M.D., author of "Advice to a Wife," etc. 16mo. Fine cloth. $1.

This invaluable work treats of the following subjects:
PART I.—INFANCY: Preliminary Conversation; Ablution; Navel Rupture; Diet; Wet-Nurse; Vaccination; Exercise; Sleep; The Bladder and Bowels.
PART II.—CHILDHOOD: Ablution; Clothing; Diet; The Nursery; Exercise; Amusement: A Poem on Childhood; Education; Sleep; The Hair of a Child.
PART III.—YOUTH: Ablution; Management of Hair; Whitening the Skin; Clothing; Diet; Air and Exercise; Amusements; Education; Household Work for Girls; Teeth and Gums; Sleep.

"Simple, practical, intelligible."—*Philadelphia Evening Bulletin.*
"It is full of sound, practical common sense."—*The Household.*
"There is a quiet simplicity and attractiveness about the book which will induce

any woman, and especially if she be a mother, to read it through at one sitting, and thereafter to retain it always for consultation and advice. We are more than pleased with it."—*St. Louis Times.*

Maternal Management of Infancy. For the use

of Parents. By F. H. GETCHELL, M.D. 16mo. Cloth. 75 cents

"We warmly recommend it for its good sense, clearness and brevity."—*The Phila. Press.*

"This little work is deserving the careful attention of all entrusted with the management of infants."—*The Inquirer.*

Dictionary of Medical and Surgical Knowledge,

and Complete Practical Guide in Health and Diseases, for Families With 140 Engravings. One handsome 12mo vol. of 755 pages Half Roxburgh, $2.50.

The Editor of this volume has brought the experience of more than *thirty* years of active practice, and over *forty* years of

professiona. study, to the task of preparing this work.

www.ingramcontent.com/pod-product-compliance
Lightning Source LLC
Chambersburg PA
CBHW030612270326
41927CB00007B/1141